The KENNEDYS
OF HOBOKEN

BY JANET KENNEDY
MURPHY

AND GREG HAYES

Published by Greg Hayes
Santa Clarita, CA, U.S.A.

Printed in the U.S.A.
© 2019 Greg Hayes
All rights reserved

Library of Congress Registration Number: TXu 2-148-465
ISBN 978-0-9969315-1-9 (biography)

TABLE OF CONTENTS

Dedication — I hope all who read this enjoy it as a window to our past and are inspired by it. — Janet Kennedy Murphy

CHAPTER 1

HOBOKEN

This is the story of the Hoboken Kennedys, and as the youngest child of Agnes and Patrick Kennedy it is my honor to tell our story.

New York City may have "East Side West Side, All around the town," but my hometown has one all its own, as in:

HOBOKEN

"OH, I WAS BORN IN HOBOKEN
H-O-B-O-K-E-N
WHERE THE GIRLS ARE THE FAIREST
AND THE BOYS ARE THE SQUAREST
OF ANY OLD TOWN THAT I KNOW
OH, TAKE ME BACK TO HOBOKEN
OUT WHERE THE HUDSON FLOWS
IN ALL KINDS OF WEATHER
WE'LL STICK TOGETHER
IN H-O-B-O-K-E-N"

Real corn, but we always got a kick out of it. If I was a musician I would put the melody down, but the best I would ever be able to do is to hum it, which wouldn't help much. There are a few other versions but this is my favorite.

Hoboken is known as the Mile Square City, since it is roughly a mile in any direction. It is a small city that is bordered on the east by the Hudson River, with Manhattan directly across the river. It was, for all its small size, an industrial giant. Hoboken hosted Lipton Tea, American Can, Tootsie Roll, Maxwell House Coffee, Keuffle &

Esser Manufacturing, Pencil Factory, Bethlehem Steel, Todd Shipyards, Lackawanna Railroad, and many other manufacturing complexes.

It is also home to Stevens Institute of Technology, which was the first college of mechanical engineering in the United States. It was founded on a bequeath from Edwin Augustus Stevens and remains today as one of the foremost institutes of its kind. The campus is strikingly beautiful overlooking the Hudson River, with a beautiful view of Manhattan as its backdrop.

Hoboken, around the turn of the 20th century, was considered by the elite of New York City as the place to go to cool off in the hot summers. Elysian Field was a meadow-style picnic area that overlooked the Hudson River. Residents of the city would take the ferry across the river, carrying their picnic baskets with them, and spend the day playing games on the cool grass and enjoying the goodies they brought along. This, of course, was before the days of the industrial takeover of the city. It eventually became a less than desirable place to live after that happened. On June 19, 1846, Elysian Park was the site of the first official baseball game ever played! The New York Nine beat the Knickerbocker Club 23-1.

In the 1930s, there were just about 60,000 residents. It was an industrial town where living in crowded conditions was an everyday part of life. There were a few parts of town, mostly on the northeast side, that were very pleasant and attractive areas that belied the normal makeup of the city. In the less affluent neighborhoods, apartment buildings were the norm. I use the term "apartments" with tongue in cheek since they were mostly cold-water flats with little or no amenities.

The city was pretty much divided along ethnic lines, with the Irish living to the east of the central street of Willow Avenue, and the Italians residing to the west of Willow. There was a smattering of other ethnic groups, but the city was essentially composed of these two cultural groups. The city

6

was also primarily Roman Catholic, with five or six churches serving the spiritual needs of the people. Most of them offered parochial schooling with nuns teaching on an everyday basis in every classroom. There were other churches and synagogues in this small area including a Hebrew School on Willow Avenue opposite one of the Catholic schools. We all seemed to get along well together, with everyone respecting everyone else's beliefs.

Neighborhoods were composed of "blocks," which were areas bounded by one street on the north, one street on the south, one street on the east, and one street on the west. Generally, almost everyone knew everyone else on their block. Kids played with other kids on their block and usually "taking a walk" when we were kids consisted of going around the block.

Each block usually had, in their immediate vicinity, every shop necessary for everyday living. In our neighborhood there was a grocery store, a butcher shop, a fish shop, a chicken shop, a greengrocer, a bread bakery, a sweet bakery, a pharmacy, a barbershop, at least one saloon, a flower shop, a shoemaker, and one block away, an undertaker. There were restaurants that sold strictly Italian, or strictly fish or what have you. There were pizza places that made the best pizza I've ever had. There were "candy stores" that sold penny candies, ice cream, cigarettes, cigars, and newspapers. Our block even had a men's haberdashery and a notions store, which sold everything from needles and thread to handkerchiefs and hosiery.

This was our neighborhood and aside from school and church, we normally spent most of our time there. It was our world and since we knew nothing else, we loved it.

CHAPTER 2

HOBOKEN KENNEDYS

Italian Barrones and Irish Kennedys

Our family began with an Italian-Irish marriage of Italian Agnes Barrone and Irish Patrick Joseph Kennedy on March 16, 1919 in Hoboken. Both of their parents immigrated to the United States in the late 1800s as part of a huge influx of Italians, Irish, and Germans who passed through Ellis Island, New York. These immigrants faced language barriers, mistrust, poverty, and even religious persecution.

Women who worked outside the home found hazardous jobs as factory workers in dark sweatshops, while men often had jobs as unskilled workers on municipal projects. They were paid low wages and lived in tenements, which were the lowest tier of housing. They often lived in crowded and unsanitary conditions, especially when as many as 10 to 12 people might share one room. Catholic immigrants also faced a rise in nativism supported by white, middle- to upper-class, American-born Protestants who worked to restrict their political, economic, and social rights.

Mother's Family

Mother's fraternal grandparents were born in Genoa, Italy sometime in the mid 1800's. Her grandfather was Charles Barrone, and her grandmother was Louisa Isola. They were married in Genoa, Italy. Her grandparents were a wealthy Italian family, and Charles was in the imported liquor business.

The family left the Genoa area in the 1870's and moved to Buenos Aires, Argentina where Mother's father James was born. He was the oldest among two boys and six girls. When James was quite young, they moved from Argentina to the United States and settled in New Orleans. At the age of 12, James was a cabin boy on the Robert E. Lee running on the Mississippi River.

Later James met a girl named Cella and they had two sons, Charles and Dominick. Charles died as an infant. Cella died after Dominick was born and so her sister raised him for a short time.

When his family settled in New Orleans, James purchased a large plot of land in the French Quarter. Eventually, the city decided they wanted to have a parcel of that land and our grandfather donated the area to the city of New Orleans. In gratitude for his generosity, the city named a street in his honor, Borone St., which means Baron. I don't exactly know why there is a difference in the spelling of the names but it is named for him.

James moved to Hoboken with his parents and a few years later married twenty-year-old Amelia Rose Raffo, who was born in Hoboken on August 6, 1878 (the same birthday as my sister Patty's first grandchild Jenny). She was baptized in Our Lady of Grace Church. Mother always remembered the date, church, and city of every family sacramental event.

Our grandparents were married on January 10, 1900 and Mother was born on November 5, 1900 and later baptized in St. Francis Church in Hoboken. When Mother was eight years old, her parents bought a lovely house. Her grandmother Louisa Isola and half-brother Dominick came to live with them as her grandfather had since passed away. Mother considered her Grandmother Barrone to be the sweetest person on earth. Grandmother Barrone loved her grandchildren and they loved her.

We know very little about Mother's maternal grandparents Benedict Raffo and Maria Podesta but they were also both born and raised in Genoa, Italy. They moved from Genoa to Manchester, England and then to Hoboken. Grandfather Raffo was very active in St. Francis Church, so that is why Mother was baptized there.

Daddy's Family

Grandpa Patrick Kennedy, Daddy's father, was born in Tipperary, Ireland and immigrated to the United States at age sixteen. He settled in Hoboken and went to work constructing the tunnels under the Hudson River connecting New Jersey and New York. Eventually he became a police officer and once was shot and wounded. He remained on the police force until his death. His badge number was #41 and it was given to Daddy when he joined the police force. After Daddy's death, the PD retired the number.

Daddy's mother was Elizabeth Sheridan. We are not sure exactly where she was born, but she was raised in Massachusetts and moved to Bayonne, New Jersey to live with her aunt Margaret McHugh when she was young. There she met Grandpa Kennedy and they were married in 1882. She was the great-great-grandniece of Philip Sheridan, the hard-driving Civil War general who defeated the Confederates in decisive 1865 campaigns that helped end the war. After settling in Boston after the war, General Sheridan was denied the chance of running for the Presidency of the United States because he was born onboard ship coming from Ireland. As a result, it couldn't be proved if he was born within the three-mile limit that was necessary to show he was a citizen of the United States.

Although he denies saying it, Philip Sheridan is credited with the terrible saying "The only good Indian is a dead Indian." His greatest compliment came from his wife. In 1875, as a forty-four-year-old widower, he had married twenty-two-year-old Irene Rucker. He died in 1888 and she lived until 1958. From the time of his death until her own death, she lived in a house filled with memories of her famous husband. When it was suggested that she remarry she declared, "I would rather be the widow of Phil Sheridan

11

than the wife of any living man.

Grandma Sheridan Kennedy and Patrick Kennedy met, fell in love, and were married in 1882. Their first child, Edward, was born, and baptized in St. Henry Church in Bayonne, New Jersey. They then moved to Hoboken, where Daddy was born on December 23, 1890 as the eighth of nine children. He was baptized in Our Lady of Grace Church in Hoboken.

Mother thought of Grandma Kennedy as a very sweet, loving person who was like a real mother to her. It was very sad when Grandma Kennedy died of ammonia, technically known as 'hyperammonemia.' That is what they called it back then when there was too much ammonia in the blood, usually caused by a liver or kidney problem.

Strange as it may seem, Grandpa Kennedy was a grouch but for some reason he was very fond of Mother. Grandpa Kennedy had been away from the Catholic Church for over thirty-two years, but Mother was a big influence on him returning to his faith. She eventually brought him back to the Catholic Church when he developed cancer later in his life. When he was nearing the end, Mother spoke to Father Fitzpatrick and he visited him. Grandpa Kennedy went to confession, received communion every week, and remained devoted to his faith until he died.

Growing up and raising a family in Hoboken

When Mother was eight years of age, she received a beautiful piano for her birthday, which became a family piano. She studied for eight years and played very well. She still had the piano when she married Daddy but sadly had to get rid of it when they had children because they needed the room.

In Union City, New Jersey, west of Hoboken, was the Vitagraph Studios. It was the most prolific American film production company, producing many famous silent films until Warner Brothers bought it in 1925. Mother loved to go there and watch the making of major silent films. To get there easily, they would go to the railroad tracks in Hoboken and from there climb the 100 steps to the studio.

One day, when she was about twelve years of age, she and some friends were watching the filming of The *Perils of Pauline* (one of the greatest silent films of all time). She was just thrilled to see the famous female star Pearl White, as well as handsome leading male stars Creighton Hale and Edgar Kennedy (no relation).

While standing there, the casting director asked her if she wanted to be in the movie. Because Mother was tall for her age with long black braids, she was the right type to take the part of an Indian maiden.

She couldn't get home fast enough to get permission to be in the great movie. However, her parents were shocked. Her father, a detective sergeant on the Hoboken police force, sat her down and said, "Agnes, I never raised a hand to you, but if I find out you are going to Union City, I will break your legs so you can't get there. Those actors are not very good people. We arrest them for drunkenness in Hoboken every night. I don't want you near them." Her movie career was nipped in the bud!

Mother was a very good tennis player and bragged that she won the high school championship against the best player, Lulu Shlicting. Lulu was sick over her loss and said she lost because Mother confused her with her left hand serve.

In June 1916, before the United States entered WWI, an ammunition dumper in nearby Bayonne was blown up. It was called the Black Tom Explosion. Her father was sent by the United States government to help Major MacKinney find the German organization responsible. Her father was very suspicious about a German druggist named Schultz who had his pharmacy across the street from our home. The day after the explosion, Mr. Schultz put an American flag in his window. I don't know how my father and Major MacKinney did it but they found out Mr. Schultz was indeed one of the many responsible. It was a proud moment for him.

Grandfather Barrone would soon deal with a tragedy from which he would never recover. His beloved Amelia Rose, Mother's mom, suffered three strokes from high blood pressure. Her first was in early 1914 and then she lived for two years as a bed patient. Grandfather Barrone loved her dearly and was so heartbroken he spent as much time as possible with her and nursed her even though they had round-the-clock nurses.

Grandmother Barrone died on Friday, October 13, 1916 at the way too young age of 38 of edema/dropsy. Mother was sixteen, her sister Maria thirteen, and her half-brother Nick almost nineteen. They eventually got a housekeeper, Mrs. Purdy, and a janitor to help them. However, Grandfather Barrone's grief over the death of the love of his life caused him to become a heavy drinker. Although he remained good to his children, it got so bad that he almost lost his mind.

Mother grew up to become a strong, independent woman. After Mother graduated from high school in 1918, Major MacKinney gave her a job on Pier 4 in the bookkeeping department at the Port of Embarkation, where soldiers left to go to fight in Europe. Although she wasn't quite eighteen years old, she was very good at math and was the only girl in an office with twenty men. Outside her window was a ship they captured from Germany. It was formerly the Fatherland but later called the Leviathan. When President Wilson came back from his trip to negotiate a peace treaty abroad, Mother was standing next to him on Pier 6. All the piers were under government sentries so people had to have passes to get in and out of the piers. She was fortunate to have one that day.

Mother and Daddy met towards the end of World War I. When they first started dating, Daddy was a play cutter at Fletcher's Shipyard. Because of his work during World War I, he was exempt from service. Mother was working on Pier 4 when they met.

Mother's marriage to Daddy was complicated from the beginning. They had been dating without the knowledge of their fathers, who disliked each other and would not have approved. In addition, Mother's Italian father disliked Daddy because he was Irish and because his family was poor compared to her family.

But there was more to Grandpa Barrone's dislike of Daddy. His own father had kept another woman and he was afraid Daddy wouldn't treat Mother well. So he didn't let Mother see Daddy. Therefore, Mother and Daddy secretly dated, then eloped in Brooklyn in the Star of the Sea Catholic Church on March 26, 1919. She was only eighteen and he was twenty-seven. They continued to keep their marriage a secret for months while she continued to live at home and work for the government and he lived with his parents and worked at the shipyards.

When she conceived her first baby, she started living with Daddy and his parents. There was a shortage of apartments due to soldiers returning from service in WWI so they couldn't find a place to live. Mother's father was furious when he found out. He angrily disowned her and refused to have anything to do with her.

The death of her mother, her father's drinking, and her secret marriage was really hard for her. They finally got their own apartment together but events that were even more difficult lay ahead of them. On March 29, 1921, Mother gave birth prematurely and shortly thereafter lost her first baby, Edward Sheridan. On December 30, 1922, she was pregnant again but also gave birth prematurely and soon lost her second son, Patrick Edward. Mother and Daddy were heartbroken, and their pain was so overwhelming that they decided they would have not any more children.

At the wake for one of the babies, Mother's father came and apologized for his treatment of them and they were reunited. They were all heartbroken over the loss of the babies and Grandpa Barrone never forgave himself for the hurt he inflicted on Mother and Daddy.

Thankfully, the hurt gradually subsided and hope was restored. Mother did get pregnant again and on February 16, 1924, Mildred came along. Mildred was born at 403 Adams

Street, nine months after they moved there. She was Daddy's pride and joy! They called her Princess and after so much heartache, they counted their blessings and cherished their baby girl. Frank came along two years later in 1926, Patty six years later in 1930 and three years later I was born in 1933. After losing two children, Mother was grateful for her "living children," as she called us. When we were all tots she took us to Mass every morning, and continued until we went to Catholic school and went with our class. Tragically, though, there would be more heartache at the loss of another child years later.

Before Mother had any "living children," they lived at 308 Madison Street. Daddy was working nights for the Jersey Central Railroad. Mother usually went to Mass in the morning at St. Francis Church on Third and Jefferson Street. She would then come home and prepare Daddy's breakfast, then hang out the window looking for Daddy to come home. She could spot him coming two blocks away.

At one point, Mother contracted ammonia and was bedridden with no one to care for her. Daddy had to work, so her cousin, Lorrette Palihnick Judge, who lived in Jersey City, came every day to take care of her and they hired a janitor to take over at night. She was very close to Lorrette. Lorette and her sisters and brother were more like siblings than cousins. With their help she fully recovered.

Mother would fix Daddy eggs and toast each morning and Daddy also liked to have cookies for breakfast. One Easter Sunday, Mother returned from Mass and prepared breakfast for Daddy. A knock came at the door and a middle-aged man asked for help. Mother and Daddy invited him in for breakfast. He was poorly dressed but clean and had a beautiful look in his eyes. He ate, graciously thanked them, and left. Mother asked Daddy to see where he went, while she looked out the window. No one ever saw him after he left the house. Mother often wondered who he was, and where he came from. She came to believe he came from God.

Mother also believed that Saint Anthony of Padua

miraculously blessed her. It was a Tuesday in June of 1930 and she was making a novena to Saint Anthony. That Tuesday was a hot, humid, miserable day and she was in her seventh month of pregnancy with Patty and wasn't feeling very well. She knew she wouldn't be able to get to the church to make her novena. Daddy was on the 8 a.m. to 4 p.m. shift working at Jersey Central Railroad. When he came home and saw her condition, he fed Mildred and Frank, ate his dinner (which she was somehow was able to prepare), saw to it that she ate a little, and then did the dishes and settled the house. He decided she would feel better if she sat on the porch downstairs.

They lived very close to the church. The side entrance was two blocks away. Daddy said he would take Mildred and Frank for a walk so that she could relax. Mother was sitting on the bench and looking at the church and thinking of her novena when she suddenly got the idea she could walk to church, make her novena, and get home safely.

So strong-willed Mother did get to church, but was very ill. She couldn't genuflect so she just bowed to the tabernacle, asked God's help, apologized to Saint Anthony for not being able to pray, and said "Please St. Anthony, help me and protect me."

She made it home, sat on the bench, and waited for Daddy and the two children to return. Annie Zuppa, who owned the house and rarely spoke to the tenants, came out and sat on the bench with her. She was waiting for her husband, Henry. They were going for a ride to the breezy East River on the Jersey side of the New York skyline.

When Henry came out, he said, "Let's get the hell out of here." Annie looked at Mother and invited her to go along, knowing that the cool breeze would make her feel better. Mother declined, saying that she was waiting for Daddy and the children and he would be worried if she wasn't there. Annie wouldn't take no for an answer so she asked Mrs. Casmania, another tenant, if she would tell Daddy where Mother was.

While this was going on Jimmy Servolino, who lived next door and worked nights, couldn't sleep because it was so hot. So he sat in an easy chair at the window with the screen door open. Eleanor, his wife, and Gerard, his five year-old son, were out for a walk. When Jimmy saw them crossing the street, he got up and went to open the door for them.

In the meantime, Annie took Mother by the hand to put her in the car. It took her a few minutes to convince Mother to go. In that time five-year-old Gerard ran up three flights of stairs, flew past his father, jumped on the easy chair at the living room window, and tragically bounced out of the window and landed where Mother had just been sitting! Mother didn't know what had happened because Henry drove away so fast. However, she later heard the story and that Gerard had died from the fall. Mother considered this a miracle as St. Anthony protected her and her unborn child because Gerard would have fallen right on them. Her pastor agreed that He had protected Mother and her unborn child. However, of course, it was so truly sad for Eleanor and Jimmy Servolino.

CHAPTER 3

GROWING UP IN HOBOKEN

We were living in a walkup flat on Adams Street when I was born, and even though we moved out of there when I was a baby, I can still remember having baths in the deep laundry sink in the kitchen. Then we moved to the flat that I grew up in at 422 Grand Street. We lived at the corner of 5th and Grand in Hoboken on the fifth floor of a six-story building above a grocery store. It was a fifth floor walkup, which was on the south side of the building. Our apartment was a five-room railroad flat. A railroad flat was one that had each room connected to the next without benefit of a hallway. We had to pass through each and every room to walk from the kitchen to the living-room. There were two flats on each floor and we had the inside one. There was definitely no privacy and of course poor air circulation.

The other tenants I remember were, starting on the first floor on the left as you came up the first flight of stairs, the Lupos. Opposite them on the right was the current janitor, who paid no rent because that was part of his wage. Next floor were the owners and landlords of the building, the Antisiches. They had both of the flats and when their only child, Margaret, married, they knocked out the walls between the two flats and she and her new husband moved into the second one. Next floor on the right were the Garricks. Mr. Garrick was an inspector with the police department and Frank Sinatra's godfather. Across the hall was Mrs. Napilotano, whose bothers were big shots in the Mafia. Next floor were the Haggartys on the right and our family on the left.

Only two of these families besides ours had children. The Lupos had grown children who had their own homes and one child still at home with them, Anna, who was a few years older than I was. The Haggartys had three children, all younger than we were: Margie, Trina, and Patrick. They were good neighbors who got along well with us. All of us living in the house were Catholics with the exception of the landlords. In fact, almost everyone in the neighborhood was Catholic and it seemed strange to us when we encountered people of other religions.

Our flat ran east to west with the living room being on the east and the kitchen on the west. There were no windows in our flat except for the living room and the kitchen, and one airshaft in the dining room and another in the bathroom. None of the bedrooms had windows and believe me it got hot in the summer with no air conditioning and no air circulation.

I remember just about everything about the building. Each flight of stairs was twenty steps high (I know I counted them many a time), so climbing them was a chore for older people, especially five flights. When you entered our building, you first came into a small vestibule, which had an inner locked door. Tenants had keys to this door, but others had to be admitted by pressing the tenant's buzzer and waiting for an answering buzzer, which would open the inner door. On the one wall were all the letterboxes with each tenant's name on their own box, which had to be opened with a key. Directly beneath each individual box was the doorbell that visitors had to push in order to gain admittance. After the visitor went through the interior door, usually someone in the buzzed flat would come into the hall and see who was there. In our case, since we lived on the fifth floor, we had to shout, "Who is it?" until we received the proper answer. I still don't know what would have happened if the person entering wasn't someone we wanted to see.

The kitchen and bathroom were all one area with the kitchen being L shaped. As you entered the kitchen from the dining room, the bathroom was on the right. The long part of the L was on the left and this area was where Mother had her sewing machine. The kitchen itself was fairly square. On the left were ceiling cabinets, the kitchen sink with a small window above it, and just beyond that was an enormous cooking and heating stove. It had gas for cooking, but the largest part was devoted to heating. It had a huge container which held kerosene, which was pumped into the stove, lighted and of course, gave off heat. The top of this heating area had flat, circular removable covers about the size of the bottom of a large cooking pot. These could be lifted with a special tool so you could check on the fire. They were also used to keep food simmering in the cold weather. Many a morning I remember getting up and running to the stove to warm up while I dressed, since it was usually the only heated space in the apartment.

Next to the stove was the boiler. This water heater had to be lit before you could have hot water. It ran on gas and it had a handle on the bottom that had to be turned to get the gas on. You then had to open a narrow door, light a match, and hold it to the burner until it ignited. Then you had to remember to turn it off since it had no safety device on it. Either turn it off or it would blow up!

On the connecting wall was a large window that overlooked an open area between our building and the next one. This was where all the laundry-drying lines were stretched. All the lines were on pulleys so you could push the wet laundry out to dry and then pull it in to fold. The pulleys were attached to telephone poles and who climbed up them to put the pulleys in place I really don't know, but can you imagine the men having to climb a sixty-foot pole to hang some pulleys?

On the right wall next to the window was a dumbwaiter to send things up or down to the first floor. We rarely used it although I found it a lot of fun. Sometimes the oilman would put the oilcans on the dumbwaiter and haul them up to us. I guess it was pretty unreliable because Daddy would usually carry the oil upstairs. I never realized how strong he must have been because each oilcan held five gallons and he carried two of them up five flights of stairs. I always wanted to climb into that dumbwaiter and lower myself down just to see what it felt like, but of course, I never did. I knew I'd be walloped for even thinking about it.

Next to the dumbwaiter was a freestanding metal storage cabinet which held the broom, dust mop, ironing board, dishes, and other supplies that didn't fit in the regular cabinets, since there were very few of them. Next to that was our kitchen table, which had wooden legs and framework but the surface was some type of yellowish brown metal with a flowery design on it. It had pull-out leaves in order to accommodate all six of us. When not in use, the leaves were pushed back into the table and it consequently took up a lot less room. We did everything on this table since there was absolutely no counter space. We listened to the radio there while we did our homework, read books, and just generally hung out in the kitchen.

The room next to the kitchen was the dining-room, where we spent a great deal of time. It had a window which opened to an airshaft, and so was usually closed. On the opposite side of this wall was a French door which was intended to shut off the kitchen, but we never closed it to my recollection. In the corner that this door created was a rather small table, which held the telephone when we finally got one.

On one wall was a china closet, which housed my grandmother's china and such. We had a very large dining table, which could sit ten with no problem. At holiday time, we had family and friends who came for dinner on a regular basis. On the opposite wall was the buffet, which was a massive piece that held table linens and the silver, etc. The wall leading out to the hallway held the entry door, then the door into the first bedroom, and next to the door was a wall with a rather large opening much like a window, although it didn't connect with an outside wall. Why it was there always bothered me because it never made sense.

Under this window was a commode, which we called a server, which was used mostly for storage. Under the table was a beautiful Oriental rug with red as the predominate color. On the walls was a flowery wallpaper with red cabbage roses each outlined in a scroll pattern, which was a very popular style paper in those days. To this day, I remember putting that paper up, and what a chore it was pasting and cutting it and wondering if we would ever get done. In the corner adjoining the kitchen was a window, which overlooked the vent area. In this corner, Mother had her chair, which resembled a sleigh in a way. The back was curved and so was the seat. There was an adjustable floor lamp behind the chair and this was where my mother usually sat when she wasn't sewing. She read the newspapers a lot, liked to do crossword puzzles, and she was addicted to detective magazines, which she bought as soon the latest ones hit the stands. They contained gory depictions of murders and mayhem, how the police solved the cases, etc., and she ate this stuff up.

Next to her chair was a beautiful secretary to write on. This held books and other reading materials. I used to love to read these books and one I remember particularly was Tom Brown's School Days. There was also a book about Fu Manchu, which was a sort of mystery, which I read and, I suppose, started me on my love of mystery novels.

In the first bedroom, which was very small, there was a built-in closet with drawers underneath. Next to the closet was a dresser and mirror and that was about all that could fit. A double bed was in the far corner. The furniture was very heavy mahogany and very dark. The bedposts had pineapple carved medallions on the very top. This was originally my parents' bedroom, but after Mildred moved into the nurse's home this was where Patty and I slept.

The second bedroom was my parents' room. They also had a double bed and dresser. Daddy had a chifferobe in which he kept his uniforms and dress suits and other clothing. Shoes fit on the bottom so that when he got ready for work everything was handy. They also had a dresser and mirror, a bedside table for Mother's books, and a large reading lamp in the room. While Mildred was still home, she and Patty slept in the double bed and I had a youth bed, which was under another window that didn't look into anything but the parlor. Crazy huh?

The parlor was the last room in the flat. There were two very large windows in the east wall and what a view from the fifth floor. The waterfront, Manhattan, the Empire State Building, the Chrysler Building, etc. were spread before us. I never really appreciated this view when I was a kid, I guess because I grew up with it. I suppose I took it for granted.

This room was a lovely room, with beautiful furnishing. There was a medium-blue couch on one wall with end tables along each side. On another wall was a red wing chair and in the corner of that wall was a darker blue chair with a matching ottoman. Between these chairs stood another kerosene heater, but unlike the one in the kitchen, it had fairly modern lines and was a very light brown color.

This room also had an Oriental rug, red with multi-colored patterns, and the same red cabbage rose wallpaper as the dining room. Behind the blue chair was a closet that we rarely used. It held the vacuum cleaner, out-of-date clothes, and the Christmas lights and ornaments. The blue sofa was a convertible couch and this was where Frank slept. This piece was unusually pretty, upholstered with clean lines. The bottom of it pulled out and revealed a trundle bed, mattress and all. The cushions on the sitting area could be turned over, and they too were covered with the same material as the mattress and could also be used as a sleeping area. Daddy slept on the trundle when he worked the midnight shift so he wouldn't be wakened by the noise in the rest of the house.

When the winter months rolled around, generally shortly before Thanksgiving, Mother would send for the rugs, which had been stored for the summer. Out came the heavy draperies along with the valances and some sheers. The

24

drapes for the dining room were brocade in a medium green and were absolutely beautiful. Mother had made them, as she made so many things, and I don't think I have ever seen any quite like them since. She had a good eye for decorating and the house showed it.

In the parlor, the drapes were exactly the same except they were a medium blue brocade and ran across the entire windowsill. The rug and drapes made the house feel very warm and cozy. I remember on days that the weather made it almost impossible to go out and play, I would snuggle up in the wing chair and read. I loved those days because my books took me away to another place and I would become entirely engrossed in them.

One flight above our flat was the roof. Sometimes when it was stifling hot, we kids would climb those stairs and go out on the roof for some fresh air. We were now six stories high but it never fazed any of us. The cool breeze coming off the river was wonderful. We couldn't take advantage of it at ground level because all the tall buildings prevented the breeze from getting to us. It was great while it lasted but eventually Mother caught us up there and ordered us down.

Outside the kitchen was the fire escape. We had to climb out the window to access it for anything needed, including hanging wash and washing the kitchen window. In the summertime, Mother closed and locked all the windows so there was never a breath of air stirring in the house; no air conditioning, no fans, nothing. All of us would swelter in the heat and at night our sheets would get absolutely wet with perspiration. It was impossible to sleep. Sometimes Patty and I would sneak out on the fire escape with our pillows and cool off until we were so afraid that we would be caught that we eventually went back to our bed. We never knew why Mother was so afraid to leave the windows open; I always thought if a burglar was going to break in somewhere, it sure wasn't going to be five flights up.

On the ground level and on the corner below us was Lupo's grocery store. The entrance door was set in the corner so that it faced both Grand St. and Fifth St. It was a typical Italian grocery with cheeses hanging from the ceiling as well as salamis and other sausages. As you entered the store, directly on the right was a huge galvanized tub containing baccala, which was dried fish, cod I think, which was soaking in a salt solution. It was very popular and people bought it on a regular basis. It stunk to high heaven and if we ever ate it I don't remember. There was a pickle barrel and a refrigerated counter where you could purchase variety lunchmeats cut to order.

On the walls were canned goods, plus all the other normal staples. When we were "sent to the store," we carried a list which we gave to Mr. Lupo or one of his sons, either Rocky or Angelo, who worked in the store on a regular basis. They would take the list and the items off the shelf and place them on the counter. They would then add them all up by hand, bag them, and then put the amount on our account, which would be paid once a month. That way if the money was tight you could get what you needed and pay it off at the beginning of the next month. They had a cash register which was used when people paid in cash, but normally they were so good at addition they didn't need the register.

Lupo's also roasted coffee several times a week. There was a roaster in the back room, the coffee beans were poured into this machine, and the heater turned on. The store had plate glass windows throughout and this roaster was directly behind one of these windows where everyone could observe the process, including all of us kids. We would watch the cylinder turn over and over and as the beans started roasting the aroma would permeate the air. I'm sure the Lupos had the minds of promotional agents, because the aroma of that coffee must have made many mouths salivate and bring those people into their store for food purchases.

Mr. Lupo was a very small man who spoke with a heavy Italian accent and was all business. However, he didn't like kids in his store, watched them with his eagle eye, and never hesitated to yell at them if he thought they were out of line or even throw them out of his store. His son Rocky was a very large man, probably in his thirties, who was married with a couple of young kids. I remember that he had very curly dark hair and was usually pretty even-tempered. Angelo, his other son, was my favorite though. He was smaller than his brother was and a bit younger. He also had dark hair but his was wavy instead of curly and if I remember correctly, he had a small mustache. He was funny and always teased us. He loved kids and made it no secret. He was usually singing and fooling around with us until his father caught him and then he would wink and go back to work. All of them wore butchers aprons and Mr. Lupo was never without his hat, so in all my memories that's the way I see them.

The candy store was on the opposite side of our building. At first, a very heavy Italian man who was very intimidating owned it. He kept a large, refrigerated Coke machine in front of his store. This didn't operate as they do nowadays. This one was a large rectangular boxlike machine with a pull-up door on the top. The drinks sat in icy water and once the lid was lifted you would simply reach inside, select your drink, and close the lid. It was operated more or less on the honor system because you were supposed to put a nickel into the slot and then take your Coke.

Some of the neighborhood kids would try to swipe a Coke out of the machine, especially on hot days, but this Italian guy usually caught them and he would chase them away from the store. As soon as he went inside those kids would come back, stand in the doorway, and chant, "Fat, Fat the water rat can't catch us cause he's too fat" and then they would run for their lives while the poor man chased them again. It was mean spirited of the kids and I have to admit I did it once but it made me feel so bad that I never did it again. At the same time, it was always funny too.

I was pretty small at this time so I don't remember when the candy store changed hands, but after a while Mr. and Mrs. Giganti became the owners. They had four kids who all worked in the store. Mr. Giganti was a tyrant who ruled his house and store with a heavy hand. His children couldn't go to the movies, listen to the radio, or read comic books because these things were evil, and only sinful, immoral people partook of such things. His daughters were not permitted to date because he believed in the way things were done in Italy, where you betrothed your daughter to the son of a good friend when they were babies. Therefore, his girls were promised since birth and there was no reason for them to go out with anyone else.

I remember when the oldest girl, Connie, was eighteen and was getting married. She had never seen her espoused since he lived in Italy. The entire wedding was planned, her gown bought and the church reserved, before she ever laid eyes on the groom. They were married three days later and she had no say about it one way or the other. Fortunately for her, he wasn't a bad looking guy, but who knows what he was like.

His other daughter, Nina, was terrified of the idea of marrying a stranger. She was about sixteen when she told Patty and me that she'd rather die than get married as her sister did. She was serious about getting away somehow and we felt so sorry for her.

The boys didn't fare much better. The older boy was Cosmo, who was my age (thirteen or fourteen), and one of my best friends. He didn't have much time for play or doing anything except go to school and work in the store. Occasionally, he could come out on a summer evening and sit outside the store and that's when we would talk. One day he was terribly upset and crying. When I asked why he was so unhappy, he told me that his father had made a decision that he, Cosmo, would become a priest and that the father was arranging to send Cosmo to a seminary. Cosmo didn't want to be a priest and especially didn't want to go to the seminary. He was terrified of having to leave his family at such a tender age but didn't know how to get out of it. Needless to say, Cosmo was shipped off to the seminary.

The youngest son, Sally, was too young, maybe eleven, for such plans, but he was the apple of his father's eye and could do no wrong. I don't remember what happened with Sally because once I started high school, at age thirteen, I was too involved in other things to notice.

The mother of this family was a very small woman. She looked as though she was quite elderly, although she must have been only in her late thirties, considering she was married early in life and her eldest child was only a teenager when I first encountered her. She dressed all in black including stockings and the babushka she wore constantly. She was extremely meek and submissive. Her husband treated her as a servant and ordered her around as though she was nothing more than a drudge. Her children told us that their mother was not permitted to sit at the table and eat until their father had eaten, then the children, and finally she could eat, if there was enough left. Sometimes if the husband had friends over, she didn't eat at all but spent the time serving them and then cleaning up. How these women could put up with this treatment is hard for me to fathom. I guess they never knew any other lifestyle.

Since we didn't have a telephone we had an arrangement with Mr. Giganti to have our phone calls come to his store. He would then send one of his children to ring our bell and then let us know that we had a call. Of course, we went immediately to their phone booth to answer. This went on for several years until we finally got a phone of our own. I'm sure that Mother paid something for this service, since I can't see Mr. Giganti doing this out of the goodness of his heart.

Like all the candy stores, this one had a showcase that featured all the types of penny candy. There were scads of it, and making a decision was mind-boggling and required a very careful assessment of the lip-smacking assortment. Of course, whoever was waiting on us usually got rather annoyed waiting for us to spend our penny or two, but eventually we selected our favorites. These were placed in a small paper bag, which we guarded with our lives as we tried to find a place to eat our goodies without sharing them with the rest of the kids. When our parents were going to be gone for an evening, Patty and I were given a nickel to spend for candy. This was usually on a weekend when Mother had a meeting and Daddy was working. Patty and I would go to a candy store around the corner from us, since Mr. Giganti's prices were not as good as this store's prices. We would make our selection and take our booty home. We would turn the radio on and sit at the kitchen table with our candy spread out in front of us. Oh, what delights!

There would be an entire package of Mary Jane's, which were peanut butter flavored caramels. These would last almost all night since they were chewy and we'd try to make them melt before we chewed them. Then there were buttons, which were multi-colored and multiflavored drops of candy stuck to a long strip of waxed paper. There were Hooton bars, which were blocks of chocolate with peanuts inside. These cost two cents so we really had to decide if it was worth the cost. Patty loved these bars and she usually bought them. My favorite was licorice, and so I would get a long rope of it. I could go on and on but you get the picture. We could get a whole bag of candy for five cents, sit, listen to the radio, and have candy to last the entire evening.

The front of our building faced Fifth St. and so we had Lupo's on the corner, next to the stoop (stoop was the local name for the steps entering the building) going into the vestibule of the house, then another store owned by the Lupos which was used only for storage. Next to that was the candy store, after that was the barbershop, and so on until the corner of Adams St. and Fifth, which housed the corner saloon.

Across the street on the opposite side of Fifth was the local public school and just beyond that was a store, which had been taken over by a men's club where the neighborhood men used to hang out to play cards and drink. Next to that was the greengrocer, LouLou, who was a first class character and lots of fun. We used to have a picture of LouLou standing in the doorway of his store, holding up a melon in one hand and waving with the other, and another picture of Daddy and LouLou together just in front of the store. I can't remember what happened to Loulou, but I do know that he gave up the store and moved away. I always missed him because he was such a clown.

On the east side of Grand St. and directly across the street from Lupo's was the butcher shop. The Della Fava brothers owned the shop. It was a good-sized store with sawdust on the floor and a large butcher-block cutting table directly behind the showcases. Whenever we would go there, one of the Della Favas would give us children a hot dog, called a "frankfurter," to eat while waiting on Mother.

Very little meat was on display since most of their customers wanted their meat "fresh." The showcases were usually stocked with cold cuts, hams and cheeses, which were cut to order. The shop never carried any chicken or fish since there was a poultry shop directly next door to the butcher shop on Fifth St. and a fish shop down Fifth on the opposite side.

Sometimes Mother would tell us to go over to the butcher shop and give him a note for some ground meat; nobody called it hamburger back then, and she was very specific. None of those scraps ground up in her order just some nice lean chuck and, if you don't mind Mr. Della Fava, please grind up the onion I sent with the meat. It was no problem: it was always done for a good customer.

Most of the shop owners either owned the entire building, had their apartments above the shop, or rented one of the apartments in the same building. The Della Favas must have owned their building since the brothers each lived there with their families. Nobody ever had to go a distance to their work, just downstairs and there it was.

The junior Mr. Della Fava and his wife had two children: Juney, short for Junior, who was my age, and Delores who was a little younger. Juney and I played together a lot until

31

his mother, Angie, died of cancer. I didn't realize that she was dying because people didn't tell her kids about things like that, but I knew that she was sick because she would sit by the window with her arms on the still just looking out. Mother would call over to her and ask how she was doing and Mrs. Della Fava would just shrug her shoulders and shake her head.

In the poultry shop, all the chickens were live and in cages. People would look into each cage, judging the weight and age of each chicken, and then select one to be their dinner that evening. The chicken would be removed from the cage, the head chopped off, and the chicken hung upside down for the blood to drain. As this process was performed, the dead chicken would flap its wings and move its legs. If the butcher stood it up it could sometimes run on the chopping block. We were so used to seeing this that it really never bothered us. I assure you that it certainly would now.

You could buy the chicken dressed, partially dressed, or undressed. We always bought it partially dressed, that is with just the feathers removed. We would eviscerate it at home. All of us girls learned to clean chickens at a very early age. It was never seen as disgusting to us because we grew up watching the process and didn't think much about it when it was time for us to learn. I remember seeing eggs inside the bird and usually several well-formed yolks. There was a sac of some sort that Mother would always tell us to be very careful of because if it was broken the chicken would have to be thrown out because this sac contained a poisonous material. I don't think any of us ever broke that sac since we'd have never heard the end of it if we did.

The fish store was something else. I guess since customers preferred their fish fresh the people in the fish shop kept a good bit of their stock alive. I particularly remember a tank of eels, which Italians love. The eels were always swimming around looking more like snakes than any fish I ever saw. We never ate eels, thank heaven, but I was there often when someone would order an eel. The eel was taken out of the tank, held by the tail over the shoulder of the fishmonger, and literally smashed down on a butcher block. Only the head hit the block so I guess this was an easy way to immobilize the eel so the head could be cut off. This I found rather gross and I was always happy that I didn't have to eat any of it.

All of our food was bought fresh with the exception of some canned goods and staples. Every day one of us went to the various stores to get the makings for dinner. Very little was kept in the house, since there was little storage or refrigerator space and this was true of everyone we knew.

Down on the far corner, opposite of the public school and the cattycorner to the saloon, was Sam's, another store that sold candy, ice cream, tobacco, etc. They also sold newspapers, so every evening we kids would walk over to Sam's and buy the paper.

Sam owned two harlequin Great Danes who were absolutely beautiful. I loved to go to Sam's so I could pet his dogs. They were very gentle and always seemed like giants to me. They were both harlequin Great Danes and wore huge collars with spikes jutting out of them. The dogs were never restrained and were free to walk around the store, which was rather large, and just do their thing. Nobody was ever afraid of them, at least not to my knowledge.

John, the Florist, was our neighborhood's flower shop. Everyone called him 'John, the Florist,' in the same way that we say Charlie Brown, as though it was his entire name. I don't ever remember hearing anyone mentioning his last name. Anyway, no one ever thought to go elsewhere for flowers. He did the entire block's funerals, weddings, and flowers for any and all occasions.

In addition to the stores we patronized, there were the pushcart vendors. These men had wooden, wheeled, very heavy wagon-like vehicles that they pushed from neighborhood to neighborhood. Most of them sold fruits and vegetables but, at times, some of them would bring shoes, clothing, household utensils, etc. If my mother needed something, she would holler out the living room window and tell the guy what she wanted.

All of the women yelled out their windows and it could get really loud and noisy. Some wanted to know if the produce was fresh and how much it cost. Others wanted to know where they got their merchandise from and so on. If one of us kids was available Mother would give us the money to take downstairs and pick up our merchandise. Other times, the money would be wrapped in paper and tossed out of the window where the vendor caught it. He would then bring up the merchandise or find some kid to bring it upstairs. I guess the kid got some sort of tip, but I never asked.

All of our streets were constructed of cobblestones and since wagons were pulled by horses you could hear the clop, clop of the horses coming down the street. It was always a soothing sound, I guess because the horses were never prodded to move very fast. I remember our milkman had a horse-drawn wagon and so did the iceman, the trash man, and the oilman.

Our milk was delivered to our door with the milk in quart size bottles. The cream always rose to the top and we had to shake the bottle in order to mix the cream with the rest of the milk. If Daddy was having his coffee when the milk arrived, he would pour some of the pure cream into his coffee before shaking it. No matter how many times the bottle was shaken, the cream always came to the top so the process was repeated many times. When I think of this poor milkman, climbing all those stairs to deliver milk to us, it's almost hard to fathom. But we were raised during the Depression and I suppose a job was a job.

Before we had a refrigerator, we had an icebox. Iceboxes were approximately the size of a dishwasher and had two doors on the front. The upper compartment was where the perishables were kept and the lower one housed the ice. Iceboxes were very heavy and very well insulated. Beneath the bottom of the box was a hose through which the melting ice water was drawn off. Everybody had a drip pan in place so the water would drip into it. One of us kids always had the job of emptying the drip pan and so help us if we forgot to do it.

We had an iceman who came to each of his customers to deliver their ice. He had a horse-drawn wagon and all of us kids watched for the wagon to come, especially in the summer, so we could get some ice slivers. The iceman was always in a foul mood, yelled, and waved his arms at us to get away from his wagon. We never went very far away and as soon as he picked up his ice pick, we could hardly wait for the small chunks to start flying. We'd grab the small ones and wait until he left to deliver the blocks and then we could really get some big pieces. I always felt sorry for this poor man, what with kids harassing him and having to climb stairs for hours every day hauling huge blocks of ice up and down, up and down, day in and day out.

He would go into the vestibule and ring the buzzers of his customers and when he entered through the inner door he would yell, "Iceman, any ice today, how much you want?", and the tenants would respond with their order. Most would get twenty-five or fifty pounds, and he would take all orders, go out to his wagon, and chip off the required amount. I never figured out how he knew how much each piece weighed since he didn't have any scales, but I guess it was all in his head. He would take these huge tongs, grab the chunk of ice, and haul it away. He'd bring it into each flat and put it inside the lower portion of the icebox where the cooling took place. Then he would be paid and go on his way. Whenever it's really hot and I'm looking to cool off I always think back to how wonderful those small chunks of ice felt.

I remember the garbage wagon coming to pick up the trash. Nobody called the cans garbage or trash cans. They were always ash cans and the janitor of each building was responsible for putting the cans out. The tenants took their trash down to the cellar and put it in the ash cans. Then the janitor would take the cans through a door that led from the cellar to the sidewalk outside the building and put them curbside for pickup.

We could always tell when the garbage wagon was coming because it was an open wagon and all the trash was just thrown into the bottom. We could smell it for blocks before it arrived on our street. Two sorts of white and grey horses pulled it. It was hard to tell because they were always so dirty. I remember one winter day watching the wagon come up the street. The streets were icy and very slippery. One of the horses fell and no one could get him on his feet. Finally, they realized that the poor thing had broken his leg and they got the cop to shoot him. I can still see that horse lying on the ground and me crying because they killed him.

Playtime for me was any time I could get out of the house if it wasn't raining or snowing. Most of the time Patty and I had chores to do around the house so getting outside sometimes proved difficult. When we did we'd go looking for the rest of the kids and then decide what to play. We were all very inventive since money was very tight for all our families and extras were out of the question, so games that required marbles were played with bottle caps. We would go to the candy store and ask for the used caps from the outside cooler. Then we would rummage around in the trash and look for orange rinds, pressing them over and down into the lining of the bottle caps. Since the caps came off the bottles without bending, the bottoms and sides were always flat and level, and since there was no grass or flat dirt areas the sidewalks became the playing field. Somebody usually had a piece of chalk in their pocket and the circles were quickly drawn and the play began. The bottle caps were flicked off the thumb and index finger exactly as a marble would be and the game played in the same fashion. It was fun and the boys usually became pretty proficient at it.

Another game was hopscotch, which we called hopsy. We would go around the corner to the shoemaker's store and beg him for an old heel he had taken off a shoe since we didn't have the proper equipment to play with. His shop was down about six steps from ground level and sometimes he was in a good mood and would give us the heel without any problem, but other times he was annoyed and would chase us. When that happened we would wait a minute or two and send someone else down and ask him nicely for the heel. If he was really angry he would throw the heel out the door at whichever one of us was there and we would have the heel regardless.

We played games such as Mother May I?, Red light, Green light; Wolf are you ready?, Tag, Kick the Can, Hide and Seek, and many others to keep us occupied. One game we played reflected quite a bit on what was going on in the world at that time. This game was called "War," which required a square area to be marked out in chalk on the sidewalk. The square was divided into four "territories" which were occupied by the Allies. Each "territory" had the name of one of the allies of the US and had one person standing in the middle of their territory. The enemy had a smaller box in the center of the square where one person stood. The enemy would turn around and around at the same time saying "I declare war on" and name one of the territories. The kids standing in their territory could only jump backward to what appeared to be a safe distance and the enemy could occupy a territory if he could touch someone without leaving the small center box. The enemy could lie down and stretch out if necessary and only had to touch the shoe of one of the kids to take over that territory. The enemy could then use that confiscated land to play from. The enemy usually lost and one of the other kids became the bad guy.

We also played a lot of games with balls. If anyone had one. The most popular was broomball, which was baseball without a baseball field. The play area was an intersection with the four corners becoming the bases and with the pitcher in the middle of the street. Time out was taken when a car came along. The bat was a broomstick and many a home run was hit with it. The outfield was anywhere beyond the four corners where a ball could conceivably be hit. It was a lot of fun to watch but not play because girls could never be on the teams. Between all this and jump rope and roller-skating and every ball game we could invent we kept ourselves pretty busy.

Another fun game was "kick the can." It was played exactly like "hide and seek" except everyone crowded around a can which was placed in the center of the street which was "home." Someone was chosen as "it" and that person kicked the can as far as they could get it to go and at the same time all the rest of the kids were scattering around in hiding places for "it" to look for them. "It" then placed the can back at "home" and then went off to find everyone. All the captured kids were placed in the middle of the street and couldn't do anything to get away until they were released. If someone could sneak back to "home" without getting caught by "it" he could shout, "All the, all the outs in free," and everyone who still had not been caught as well as all the captured were free again to start the game all over. If "it" caught everyone another "it" was selected, usually the first person caught.

The girls loved to jump rope and we had many different sayings to jump to. When you became proficient at jump rope with just a single rope then you went on to "Double Dutch" which required two ropes and which was pretty difficult. Patty and I became very, very good at any types of jump rope, especially "Double Dutch, and spent lots of time at it.

We were also very good at paddle ball and even impressed out children later in life with our paddle ball skills. Paddle ball is a vintage one-person game played with a paddle and an attached ball. Using the flat paddle with the small rubber ball attached at the center via an elastic string, we would try to hit the ball with the paddle in succession as many times as possible

We also roller-skated a lot. Skates at that time were long pieces of metal shaped like a shoe with clamps at the front to tighten against your shoe and straps at the back to fasten around your ankle. They could go like the wind and I became an excellent skater. When we got older, we got shoe skates and went to the skating rinks on weekends.

Our city also sponsored activity days in the summer with picnics and games, etc. They also had races and other athletic events. I usually was entered in the girl's sprints for my age group. Since I was always head and shoulders taller than the other girls I had no problem winning with those long legs.

Another activity we had was band. Daddy was a great cornet and trumpet player and he taught Mildred, Frank, and Patty to play those instruments. Why I wasn't taught also is still a mystery to me. Anyway, the city had a band for youngsters up to about sixteen years old. We were all involved in the band and since I couldn't play an instrument I became the drum major. We marched in parades and had lots of practices as I remember it. The uniforms were white with green and gold trim. The girls wore skirts and the boys slacks. They had shoulder capes, which were white with Kelly green satin lining and white overseas caps with the green and gold trim. My uniform was solid green satin with slacks and a shako in green. The jacket had gold frog closures up and down the front and the shako had gold trim. We used to have pictures of us dressed in our uniforms but they are long gone.

Speaking of Mildred and Frank, they babysat Patty and I sometimes. Mildred was great with always finding something new to show us. I'll never forget that she taught me to sing and waltz to "Little Nellie Kelly" when I was five. Frank was something else. He would pretend that we would play cowboys and Indians. He would then take a blanket, toss it over a chair, and make that a tent. He would "capture" Patty and me, tie us up, and put us in the tent. He would then lie on the couch and listen to the radio while we waited to be "rescued."

Another one of his "games" was to have us lie on the floor next to the couch and play statues. We had to be completely still and if we moved he'd punch us, not hard you understand, so we would be still and stop bothering him. One of us would be declared the best statue if we let him listen to his program so we tried hard to be still.

Mildred and Frank shared a lot of the same friends. They would give parties together and have the gang over, all from the group at Our Lady of Grace. As I said earlier, my bed was next to the living room with that silly window separating the two rooms. I can remember that these parties would wind up with them all celebrating "Mass" with candy wafers or banana slices as communion. Since all the guys were altar boys, they were all pretty familiar with the Latin and the ritual. It was very fascinating to watch this; I still have very vivid memories of these parties. Of course, they also played records and told jokes, etc. and had a regular fun party for themselves, but I always think of the "Mass" thing.

I guess my love of early forties music comes from Frank and Mildred always listening to that music and it made an impression on me. As Patty and I got a bit older, we always listened to the radio and one of our favorites was the "Make Believe Ballroom" with Martin Block as the Deejay. He played all the current music and introduced the newest recordings so we had an easy time keeping up with them.

Our church had many older guys as altar boys. Many of them were in high school and the older they became the more they were used for the more important ceremonies. We had lots of processions which were very solemn occasions and Frank and some of his buddies were usually called upon to participate. Usually, Frank would carry the book walking backwards so the priest could read the ritual prayers and his buddy, Red Hayes, would have the incense. As he swung the incense holder he would be looking straight at Frank and he would mimic singing, "Yes, we have no bananas" or some other silly song trying to break Frank up. Since the priest was also looking directly at Frank he would try his hardest not to look at Red, but sometimes it didn't work and he'd crumble. Of course, he had the riot book thrown at him afterwards and Red would get away scot-free. I know it doesn't sound very funny now, but you really had to know Red Hayes then;

he was very, very funny and he made everyone laugh, even Mother.

I always loved to read, I guess because it took me away to so many different places and adventures that I forgot lots of things that weren't such happy events. I spent a lot of time at the library and got in trouble many times for being late coming home. I still love to read and don't spend a single day without a book in my hands.

In the summer when it got really hot the firemen would open the hydrants in front of the firehouse and let the water gush out like a mini geyser to spray all the kids. Mother wouldn't permit any of us to play in the water so I don't know how much fun it could be, but it sure looked like everyone was having a great time. The closest to the water we ever got was to take off our shoes and socks and wade in the cold water running in the gutters.

Speaking of the summers, the Italian churches had their festival honoring various saints and, of course, Jesus and Mary. The statues were huge but they were carried around the streets anyway. The statue was mounted on a platform and this platform had thick logs running for probably ten feet on either side. The men would shoulder the logs and start the procession. There were perhaps eight to ten men per side and other men walked alongside of them to take over when someone got tired.

In front of the statue was an Italian band made up of about twenty men, but nobody marched or even tried to keep in step. They just sort of meandered around as a group playing terrible music, or at least that's how it sounded to me. The statue had ribbons around the neck which I always loved to read, so I liked them.

Many went on their knees when they arrived at the church and climbed the steps on their knees. The steps were usually made of rough stone and many of these women developed deep cuts and bruises.

The procession went on for at least an hour or two until they arrived back at the church, where food was being served and the band continued to play. All along the line of march, firecrackers were set off constantly until the noise was unbearable because we all had to have our windows open because of the heat. If you ever get a chance to see Godfather Two, where Vito is a young man with a young family, you will see exactly how our area was growing up. The Mafia was an everyday reality in our neighborhood.

Hoboken Cop

After working in the shipyards and railroads, Daddy became a Cop (constable on patrol) in 1937 and our neighborhood was his beat. He became a well-respected member of the Hoboken Police Department for thirty-eight years. He was loved and admired by all in the neighborhood. He carried badge # 41 ... the same number that his father wore for his thirty-seven years while on the force. He made about $2,000 a year so Mother lined his police coats because they couldn't afford to have it done professionally. His police uniform was always neat, his pants pressed, and he looked like a million bucks in his uniform.

Daddy would walk a neighborhood beat every day he worked. When we lived on Washington Street, he would start out there, then head to 14th Street where part of his job was to turn the buses around safely so they could make their trip back down Washington St. After he completed that task, he always stopped at Te'Amo store where he would pick up his favorite cigar. From there he walked to Hudson Street along the Hudson River. Across the street was the Stevens Institute of Technology and the New York City skyline.

Daddy was just such a sweet and loving father, grandfather, and overall person. All three of us girls loved him but Patty adored him the most. Patty and Daddy were very similar in so many good ways. He was also the friendliest police officer there was. But if he sensed trouble he quickly got very serious and protective and ordered that Mother or anyone else get home right away. It rarely happened but when it did, everyone knew to follow his orders because they trusted him so much.

Daddy always carried a white pearl handle, two-barrel Derringer with two chambers and two bullets. At home, he kept his gun clean and locked up. However, if he was out, he carried it with him, and if he was in New York City walking around he might lift his jacket for others to see. He would especially do that if he was with his grandchildren.

Mother wouldn't let Daddy smoke his cigars in the house so Daddy would go for a walk so he could enjoy them. He did not smoke the cigars as much as chew on them. He would walk through the neighborhood along his regular police beat. He didn't drive so he walked everywhere; that was why he was so thin.

He even walked his regular beat in the summer when he was not working because there was no air conditioning and poor circulation in the apartment. Neighbors sat on the front steps smoking or just hanging out because it was too hot inside. Daddy was so well liked and respected that people would say "Pat, how are you doing?" when he walked by. It was community policing at its best. He was like a celebrity, and the neighborhood merchants liked and trusted him.

He always seemed to know what was going on in the neighborhood and where there might be trouble. Daddy knew the owner of every bar on every corner on Hudson Street. He would ask the bartenders who needed help getting home every night. The bartender might say Anna called and wants Fred home now. So Daddy would walk Fred back to his apartment where Anna would be waiting, not always happy with Fred. People in the bars would also buy Daddy a drink, Daddy's police captain always said if you go in a bar and the house doesn't buy you a drink, then leave.

He had a favorite tavern at the corner of 14th and Washington where he would have a glass of whiskey. One time he walked in and the owner said, "Hey Pat, I have some troublemakers here. They are longshoremen from Todd Shipyards and I'm gonna call the patty wagon because they're drunk."

Daddy said, "Let me handle this. I'll take care of it." He told the guys, "I don't want to cause you any trouble so how about going across the street to the YMCA? I will get you a room and you can sleep it off." They said yes and so he booked two rooms for them at 50 or 70 cents a night. He kept them out of trouble and showed so much kindness. That was indicative of what a regular guy he was. That is why he never moved above being a police officer.

Daddy would get tickets to the Yankee games because he was a well-liked police officer. They were such good seats that they would sit by celebrities such as famous and attractive actress Lorraine Day, wife of the equally famous baseball manager, Leo Durocher. Daddy would often take his sons-in-law and grandchildren to the games with him.

In later years, when his grandchildren Jimmy and Lawrence were older, he would walk his beat with them and buy them a Tootsie Roll Pop for 2 cents or a Coke, while he had a shot of whiskey at a local tavern. He loved to give them nicknames. Jimmy was "Duke" and Lawrence was "Mulligan." Mildred's daughter Carleen was "Lady Bountiful." My Colleen was the "Village Queen."

Daddy hated to go to the dentist so he never went. Gradually he started losing his teeth. By the last five to six years of his life, he had one tooth left and of course, he had fun with that. It made eating tough but he just used his tongue, gums, and that one tooth to make it all work.

That didn't bother the grandchildren, who just loved being with him. When Mildred's kids were older and living in Plainfield, Daddy would come over and hang out with them on the porch while he smoked his favorite cigar and talked to them about life.

Jimmy, the oldest Kennedy grandchild and Mildred's oldest, had a special connection with Daddy, and they went to games together at Yankee Stadium. Jimmy would ride a bus from his home and meet his grandfather at the Port Authority bus platform at 40th St. in New York City. Daddy was a dapper dresser, and would meet him dressed to the nines in his fedora and light spring jacket. They would take the E train to 59th St. and then take the B Train to 161st St. and River Avenue where Yankee Stadium was. Daddy knew people at Maxwell House, Lipton Tea, and Hostess who really liked him and would give him good seats behind home plate or behind the third base dugout. They would see Mickey Mantle, Whitey Ford, Yogi Berra, and the other great Yankees up close as they enjoyed hot dogs and time together.

After the game, Daddy and Jimmy would leave the lower-level seats and go on the field, which was how fans left the stadium. The ushers in their red blazers would form a perimeter around the infield and direct fans to walk to the monuments in centerfield and then out the big gate behind it. Daddy and Jimmy would walk through the gate to River Avenue and then to a tavern where Daddy would have a whiskey and Jimmy a Coke. They would then go back to the Port Authority and Daddy would make sure that Jimmy got on the bus safely to go home. These were special memories and bonding times for each of them.

Years after Daddy passed, Jimmy and others noticed the smell of cigar smoke in Jimmy's house. Jimmy would tell them it was just Grandpa visiting. It was because of Daddy that Jimmy would eventually go into public service and do it so successfully and with such integrity.

Meanwhile, Mother entered politics and was elected county and city committee woman for twenty-eight years. She was also president of the Democratic Auxiliary Club for sixteen years in Hudson County along with Dolly Sinatra, mother of the famous entertainer Frank Sinatra. Mother also became a medical librarian and established libraries at Saint Mary's Hoboken and Mother Cabrini in New York. At that time, her cousin Edward Barrone Sr. had her named Committee Woman for the Third Ward, Seventh District to fill the uncompleted term of the woman who held that job and had moved.

She held that post for the next twenty-eight years until Mayor Bernard McFeeley was defeated. McFeeley was a powerful mayor because he allied himself with Frank Hague, the Hudson County political boss and very powerful mayor of Jersey City. The Fusion ticket defeated Mayor McFeeley and his Democratic machine in May 1947, and Fred De Sapio succeeded him as mayor. McFeeley died two years later while facing corruption charges.

As a Third Ward leader, Mother had an important role in the city's political machine. She acquired Democratic votes for political leaders and gave out and gained favors. Like most people in Hoboken, she was very aware of the division between the Irish and Italians, but her close involvement with those in power allowed her to work with both groups.

Frank Sinatra

The most famous person from Hoboken was Frank Sinatra, who was born in our city on December 12, 1915. He was baptized Francis Albert Sinatra on April 2, 1916 in St. Francis Church. When he was little, he used to grab a stick and sing on the streets as if he was singing into a microphone. His first actual singing performance was at a church supper at St. Ann's Church at 704 Jefferson. I should explain that many of the streets were named for the early US presidents – Washington, Adams, Jefferson, Monroe, etc.

His parents were Italian immigrants who grew up in Hoboken. His mother, Natalina Garvata, was smaller than five feet and weighed about ninety pounds, but she had a big and forceful personality. She was called "Dolly" because of her pretty face.

His father, Antonio Martino "Marty" Sinatra, was a former prize fighter known as Marty O'Brien, who was a really nice but salty guy. He later became a fire captain at Firehouse Number 5 just down the street from us. He used to sit outside and all of us kids would wander up there sometime during the day to visit him. The doors to the fire house would open and he would take us inside and put us in the cab of the firetruck or on the back where the firemen would stand and hang on as they rushed to a fire. He was a kind, gentle soul and loved us kids. I can't ever remember him getting annoyed with us or chasing us away. Weather permitting, Mother would sit with Marty on a bench in front of the firehouse and they talked a blue streak, mostly about Frank.

I had no clue he was Frank Sinatra's father and really didn't care. I liked Marty because he was so nice to us. Of course, eventually we realized who he was, but since we were a bit older and knew the Sinatra family it never mattered when he became so famous.

Patty's husband, Johnny, once went to a baseball game with Daddy at the Polo Grounds and they met Frank Sinatra's dad there. They sat down next to the Giants' dugout. The field was turtle-shaped for drainage so if you sat in the dugout you could only see the heads of the players on the opposite side of the infield.

On the way home, Johnny made a lane change and cut off a fire engine. He was pulled over and they threatened to arrest him, which firemen could do back then, but they didn't. The next day, Mother went down to the fire station. Captain Sinatra asked her, "What can I do for you?" Mother then chewed him out for twenty minutes for his guys threatening to give Johnny a ticket.

As a rare only child, Frank was good to his parents. He could be a wise guy kid and had street smarts. Occasionally, Daddy would have to chase Frank around Hoboken. He grew up in a tough Italian neighborhood so his dad taught him how to box in order to protect himself. He attended Demarest High School at Fourth and Garden Street but was expelled after forty-seven days after being accused of a prank.

Frank was a Hoboken kid who used his unique talents and some good breaks to become America's first teen heartthrob. It is funny to think of all those girls doing the Swoonatra and fainting at his concerts. When he first started out singing professionally, he used to hang out inside Leo's Grandevous on Grans Street and shoot pool. Even after he became a superstar, he would stop in town. He liked to go to

Dom's Bakery at 506 Grand where he liked things very well done and even burnt. He would have his limo driver pull up to Lenore's Home Made Chocolates at Sixth and Garden to get his favorite treat, chocolate-covered dried apricots.

Mother and Dolly Sinatra were very close friends and committee women in the Third Ward. Dolly was in the Ninth district and Mother was in the Seventh. In fact, Mother babysat Frank when he was boy. Sometimes Patty and I had to carry messages back and forth from Mother to Dolly and from Dolly back to Mother. Dolly was a foul-mouthed woman, as was her good friend, actress Ava Gardner (who later became Frank's second wife), and she had a short fuse. She cussed constantly and Patty and I were sort of afraid of her. Although she would yell at us and once threw us out of her house, she never did anything to cause us any real problems.

Mother once asked Dolly for an autographed picture of Frank Sinatra and so Dolly asked Frank for a picture. He said he didn't have one but he would the next time he saw her. The next time she saw him she asked for the picture and he didn't have one. She said to him, "Stick it up your ass." The next time he saw her he made sure he gave her the autographed picture.

I never did get to meet Frank Sinatra in person because every time he was going to be home or at the fire station, his bodyguards surrounded him. Several times, we were to meet him at his parents' home but something always interfered. Mildred met him a lot, especially when Dolly was in the hospital where Mildred was nursing. Mildred would help to sneak Frank in because his fans would surround the hospital. One time they took him out in an ambulance because the crowds were so thick.

Dolly always got a kick out of embarrassing Mother with her jokes and language. Once, when Dolly was sick and confined to St. Mary's Hospital and Mother was in the medical library there, she and Frank Sinatra would visit Dolly. One day when Frank couldn't get in to see her because the nurse wards had her on the bedpan, he made such a fuss that the nurse opened the doors, handed him the bedpan, and left. It was a riot. She was the head nurse and so she couldn't be fired for doing that.

The first time I saw Frank Sinatra perform was at the Fabian Theater. The Fabian was a movie theater but on Wednesdays, they had an amateur night. I guess I was about six or seven when he appeared and again I really didn't realize who he was. He was only beginning his career at this time and he was part of a group called "The Hoboken Boys." They performed this particular night and I have never forgotten it.

I remember Mother telling us about a time she saw Frank Sinatra and I guess he was a bit full of himself. She told him he had better not get uppity with her because there were many times she had diapered and powdered his bottom when she babysat him years before. She said he laughed and told her he was sorry if it appeared that he was being a snob because he surely remembered spending time with her.

Mother and Dolly Sinatra were so close that when Dolly was killed in a private plane crash some reporter called our house to see if Mother had been on the plane with her. When someone wrote a biography about Dolly, Mother was put out because nobody interviewed her for information about the "real" Dolly.

Because Mother was in politics, we had to live in her district, hence the Italian neighborhood. The people came to her with their problems and many times, it was trouble from the Black Hand, the old name for the Mafia. If a business was successful, they wanted to sell the owner "insurance." If the man didn't want to or couldn't afford it, the Black Hand would slip a piece of paper under their door at night with nothing on it except a picture of a black hand which, of course, was a warning to them. I never knew how it was handled or resolved but I always knew that they were bad people to be afraid of.

But Mother was very good at what she did and sometimes

corruption came from unexpected sources. At one point, Mother wanted to move elsewhere in Hoboken. The moving vans were outside bringing stuff down from the fifth floor when two plainclothes police officers came up to her and said, "Are you moving?" Mother said yes. They said, "If you move, your husband is going to lose his job." So Mother told the movers to take the furniture back up.

The reason they wanted her to stay was that Mother was so good at turning out the Democratic vote that they did not want her to leave the precinct. It was the same with Dolly Sinatra. They wouldn't let her leave either.

SCHOOL

While we had a public school directly across the street from us, we only attended it for kindergarten. After that, we went to the Catholic parochial school, Our Lady of Grace, which was just a block away. We wore uniforms that consisted of a navy blue pleated skirt, a white middy blouse (just like sailors wear) with a large red ribbon bow around the neck. We carried "school bags" exactly like briefcases, instead of backpacks. School started at 8 AM and we got out at 3 PM. Since we didn't have a cafeteria we had to go home for lunch. We made sure we ate quickly and ran back to school so we could get in some playtime until lunch break was over. There was a concrete playground surrounded by a fence where we could play dodgeball or tag or jump rope. When the bell rang, we had to line up according to class with no talking or we would have to stay after school.

The nuns were pretty strict but rarely lost their cool. We had a few who would take a ruler or a pointer and whack your knuckles if you goofed off in class. Even though they wore wimples that completely concealed their side vision, they always knew who was up to something and "BAM" the pointer would come down on your hands. It really stung but never did any damage except to our egos.

I liked most of the nuns I had in class, especially Sister Vera. She was a first class character and had a great sense of humor. I had her for eighth grade and loved being in her class. Another special nun for me was Sister Monica. She was very tall and thin and most of the kids were afraid of her, including me. She was very strict and demanded a lot out of her class. Since my mother started me in kindergarten at four, I was only five when I went into first grade and didn't turn six until the end of the school year. I was the only one who was always a year younger than the rest of the class and almost all of them picked on me and called me baby. Most of us were promoted to the next grade as classes and so I automatically had the same classmates every year, and every year they made fun of me.

When I got into fifth grade with Sister Monica, I was head and shoulders taller than my classmates and skinny to the point of being called "beanpole." At that time, my parents took us for eye exams and the doctor decided I needed glasses. I am sure all of us know that back then kids who wore glasses were geeks and were tormented and bullied unmercifully. Since I was already the object of their derision I knew that when I showed up with glasses they would have a ball at my expense.

I went to school that first day very early and didn't play in the schoolyard at all. Instead, I went to my classroom and sat at my desk. I didn't have my glasses on and I must have looked as though my world was coming to an end. Sister Monica came in and was surprised to see me in my seat. She asked me if anything was wrong and I told her about the glasses. She already knew how the other kids teased me and realized how upset I was. She told me that she would take care of it when class started and true to her word, she instructed me to put on my glasses and dared anyone to poke fun at me. She said that the ones who jeered at me would not only have to stay after school but would also have to write an essay on how to be kind to others. She then informed all of us that she also had been quite tall and gawky in grade school and knew how terrible it was to be ridiculed on a daily basis and that she would not tolerate it in her class or anywhere on the school grounds.

After class that day, she asked if I would like to be her companion when she went out in the afternoons. Nuns then had to be in pairs when they left the convent and she told me that she would find it refreshing to have one of her students accompany her. I said it was okay with me as long as my mother approved. Of course, she got my mother's permission and she took me with her many times. I always enjoyed being with her because I felt safe with her and knew nobody would dare make fun of me with her around. She knew how to deal with bullies and how to make me feel worthy.

At certain times of the year, the school put on assemblies that were like either a variety show or a little play and, of course, a Christmas show as well as a St. Patrick's Day show. Patty and I were always called upon to perform because we looked so much like twins. I remember being angels in one Christmas play where the first graders were all supposed to be asleep on the stage. We came on stage, one of us from each side, and tiptoed around the sleeping children and blessed them. Then we silently left the stage and the children awoke and were excited about the angels who had come in the night. Another time I remember was a St. Patrick's Day show where Patty and I were dressed in Irish costumes and where we danced a jig. I remember it vividly but I no longer know how to dance the jig.

When I was twelve my appendix ruptured. I was rushed to the hospital by ambulance and sent to surgery as soon as possible. I remember being in the operating room and a priest coming over to me and giving me absolution and telling me that when I woke up I would probably be in heaven with God. The church was directly across the way from the hospital and the OR had lots of high windows. I remember looking over there and seeing the cross on the steeple and not being afraid at all.

There were no drugs comparable to what we have today except for penicillin, which was discovered in 1939. It took a while for it to become an accepted drug but when the war broke out it began to be used for the troops. It was hard to get for civilians and the doctor was trying to procure some dosages for me.

Mildred was an Army nurse at Halloran Army Hospital in Long Island. When she was notified that things looked grim for me she got leave and rushed over to St. Mary's Hospital, where I was undergoing surgery. She scrubbed and joined the doctors in the OR. She had trained at St. Mary's and all the doctors and nuns knew her and our family. The doctor told her there was no hope because the infection was severe and peritonitis had already set in. In those days, it was almost unheard of for someone to survive peritonitis. I understand that the hospital obtained some of the antibiotic and, while it took a very long time, I finally recovered. This happened in June and our school was closed for summer break. Someone from the hospital notified the school and told them I had already died, so our principal sent messages to every classroom to pray for my soul and to be prepared to attend my funeral.

I was in the sixth grade then, just ready to be promoted to seventh grade. I had as my teacher Sister Margaret Delores and I thought I hated her. I was so happy to be moving on. One day, as I was recuperating, Sister Margaret showed up to visit me. She gave me the exciting (to her) information that our principal had changed her from sixth grade teacher to seventh grade teacher, so she would be my teacher the following year. I must have received the news with a disgusted face because she said that she realized it was a disappointment for me but it would all work out which, of course, it did.

Speaking of nuns and priests, my mother sewed for them and they were always in our house. They needed measurements, try-ons, or whatever. Mother made the nuns' habits and the priests' albs and surpluses. She learned how to make the habits when we were quite small. The nuns had always admired her sewing and all the clothes she made for us. One of them asked Mother to make a habit for her and Mother said she really couldn't because Sister had no pattern. Sister said that Mother was so talented that she was sure Mother could make her own pattern. Sister left an old habit with Mother and Mother took it apart piece by piece until she knew all the parts and where they fit. Eventually Mother made the habit for this particular nun and, of course, since she didn't charge but a couple of dollars, the word got around and pretty soon she was making habits for all the nuns, albs and surpluses for the priests, and any sewing the church needed.

PENNSYLVANIA

Sleeping was tough on Daddy. He worked three different eight-hour shifts so he could never get in a good sleep pattern. It was hard to sleep during the day in Hoboken because of the noise and the heat of the summer. He would work three different shifts for three weeks at a time: 4 PM to midnight, then midnight to 8 AM, and then 8 AM to 4 PM. Can you imagine trying to sleep in that summer heat and noise? People had no air conditioning and poor air circulation and slept with the windows open. There were 60,000 people living in one square mile.

But we were able to escape that. Grandpa Barrone owned a bungalow in Dingmans Ferry that was just a short walk from the Delaware River. The lot was huge and he had owned the home for years. When Mildred was four months old, Mother bought her father's house in Dingmans Ferry; I guess our family went over there for the summer to get away from the city heat. I can only remember going there briefly since we stopped going when I was four. However, I have vivid memories of the entire area, some of our neighbors, and especially the trips up there and back since I got carsick all the time. We usually went up in late June and stayed full time until it was time for school to start again. Mother took us to Pennsylvania because she wanted her children to spend the summers out of the city. Of course, Daddy had to stay in

Hoboken to work so we looked forward to his weekend visits and time with him. We didn't have a car so one of our uncles or friends drove him there.

We swam in the river (I was so little that I paddled) just about every day and I remember everyone telling me not to go near the whirlpools because they would suck me under. What a change from the city. The area was rural and beautiful. We went into town for groceries and church. Frank and Mildred would walk into the village a couple of times a week and they would bring Patty and me a lollypop as a treat. Patty and I would wait out on the road for them to come back. We had a special call, something like the Tarzan call. We would yell it out, and if they were close enough they would call back and we would run up the road to meet them. I always had a wild cherry lollypop and to this day, I can remember the taste. They were that good.

I don't remember how we got to church, but I do remember there was a policeman on horseback who was there most of the time and every once in a while he would put us little ones on his horse and lead us around a bit. What fun that was.

Our other family members would come over on a regular basis, especially Mother's brother Uncle Dommie Barrone and his wife Aunt Tessie. They were so much fun to be around. Aunt Tessie was sharp as a tack but always played the dummy and made us laugh. We all loved them so much. They didn't have any children and they were so good to us. Mother's sister Aunt Marie and her husband Uncle Jimmy Clark had two daughters, Eleanor and Virginia, who were around the same age as Mildred and Frank. They also came to the house frequently and stayed so many times we had quite a group there. They were so nice and Uncle Jimmy made me laugh a lot. I remember sitting on his lap so much of the time and just couldn't get enough of him.

The house was huge with front and back screened porches running the full width of the house, which must have been fifty or sixty feet across. The rooms all opened off the porches with the bedrooms being in the front. They didn't have a bathroom until after I was born, but even so we had chamber pots under the beds to use at night. The house was in a valley and because the mountains were so close it got very cold at night. I remember sleeping in pajamas AND a bathrobe to keep warm, so it was the opposite of our hot Hoboken nights. We used kerosene lamps to light the porches and rooms. I know that eventually Grandpa put electricity in but I don't think we used it all the time. When there were thunderstorms in the summer the clouds would pile up over the mountains and we could watch the storms moving in. We would wait until the very last minute to run into the house because we never knew if the rain would come over our area. Much of the time, we could see the rain fall across the road and even in our neighbors' yards but not in ours. It was fun to watch it rain in our yard and not in the adjoining yard or vice versa.

Grandpa had outlined the front yard with large rocks, which were whitewashed. They had to be done every summer to keep them looking nice. I know I probably didn't contribute much to the job, but Patty and I were allowed to help. Frank would turn some of the rocks over, find every kind of creepy crawler known to man under them, and then chase us with them until someone would come out to see what the ruckus was all about.

Some of the people who came to visit were close friends of our parents. One time these friends came over and brought their son with them. Frank and this other boy were out looking for some adventure or other and got into some poison ivy. The next day they were full of itchy blisters and Mother got some needles and some antiseptic and broke every blister on them. You could probably hear them yelling miles away.

Most evenings we would sit out on the lawn and just watch the stars and whatever wildlife was around. I can vividly remember the lightning bugs sparkling in the darkness. Some we would catch and put in bottles, but most of the time we just enjoyed them. In those days the lightning bugs were so plentiful it seemed that hundreds were flying around us each night. It was truly magical.

Patty's birthday is on August 12th and Daddy always made it a point to be there to celebrate. He always brought us dolls (me too) and new bathing suits and bathing caps. The caps were twisted around a white cardboard cylinder and if the cap was red, it looked exactly like a peppermint candy cane. Daddy was always so thoughtful about bringing us gifts and years after would do the same for his grandchildren. He was such a wonderful father and so loving. If one of us got sick, he always brought us something we could do in bed, like cutout dolls or sewing kits or anything like that.

One August we were waiting for Grandpa and Uncle Jimmy to bring Aunt Marie and the girls to visit us in Pennsylvania. Either they were supposed to come very late at night or early in the morning. I really think it was at night because I remember Daddy getting out of a car and Mother knowing that something was wrong because it wasn't Daddy's day off and it was early morning.

Grandpa and Uncle Jimmy had been in an accident and Grandpa went through the windshield and was decapitated. Uncle Jimmy was in critical condition but eventually pulled through. What was really eerie was that Aunt Marie and the girls had been in the car and she told Uncle Jimmy shortly after they started to turn around and go back because she had a premonition that something was wrong. He scoffed at her and Grandpa also refused to change his plans. She insisted on not going, so he dropped Aunt Marie and the girls off at their home and he and Grandpa continued on their way. Strange, huh? Mother was devastated and insisted we leave immediately to go back to Hoboken. She always said that was the one and only time I didn't get carsick on one of those trips.

Mother said she never wanted to go back to the bungalow again and we never did. I wish she had reconsidered because although I only have some memories, I truly loved the place. I never knew any of my grandparents when I was little since most of them had died before I was born, except for Grandpa Barrone and he died when I was four. I do remember him taking Patty and I to one of the family-style saloons where there was sawdust on the floors and a free lunch. Grandpa would sit us on the bar and give us sarsaparilla to drink along with whatever we were allowed to eat from the lunch table. To this day when I think of that time, I can still taste the soda and smell the beer.

CHRISTMAS

Christmas was always so very, very special, because Daddy made it so. Patty made Christmas very, very special for her children and grandchildren later on and she probably got that from Daddy. But then again, she was more like Daddy than any of us kids. I don't know why Mother wasn't into Christmas but she never was.

Daddy always selected the tree and it was usually from one of the vendors on his beat. He said that he trusted them to sell him a nice fresh tree because they knew him so well. I still remember that it took at least three of us to carry the tree home because it was so tall and heavy. Then we had to haul it up five flights of stairs and set it up in the parlor. Sometimes we had to cut the top off because it wouldn't fit any other way.

Daddy would get the light sets out and check the bulbs and then after he put the lights on the rest of us could do the decorating. He hated to have the tinsel just thrown on the tree so instead he taught us to put it on carefully so it hung down just like icicles. Mother never participated in decorating the tree and we were so used to her not being involved that we never questioned why she didn't.

Daddy, while Mother got us socks and pajamas and other practical gifts, usually bought our toy gifts. We didn't receive much back then. We might get one doll and a game. If we got a tricycle, it was always to be shared by Patty and me. It was the same thing with doll carriages and other larger toys. We learned to share and didn't complain. Mildred and Frank got things like ice skates and clothes.

On Christmas Eve, Mother would make ravioli to serve for Christmas dinner. She would place a clean white sheet on the kitchen table and cut out the pasta. Then Patty and I would put them on a tray and take them over to place on the floured sheet to dry somewhat. The sheet would be covered with the ravioli before Mother was done and we couldn't wait for Christmas to come so we could eat them.

On Christmas Day, she would stuff and roast a huge turkey and all the trimmings so we had both types of dinners for the holiday. Relatives would come and join us and we all stuffed ourselves. In those days, special days were always looked forward to because the dinners were so out of the ordinary and just like a feast. We had good food but simple cooking on normal days, but all the special baking and cooking for the holidays made us anticipate the meals as much as the gifts.

One Christmas during WWII, Frank was ready to deploy with his Marine battalion to China and told us he would not be coming home for Christmas. Mother said that we couldn't have any kind of celebration because of Frank not coming, not even a tree. We were pretty unhappy with that but no one could persuade her to change her mind. On the Sunday before Christmas, we went to church as usual. We always sat in the same place every week and shortly after the Mass started Frank walked in and surprised us all. Their deployment had been delayed and he had managed to get a short leave. When we got home and there was no tree up he was terribly disappointed and insisted we go find one. The only tree we found was about twelve feet high and probably didn't have more than a dozen branches on it. It was pathetic to say the least. We did all the decorating and it looked awful with all those empty spaces. Mildred got the bright idea to get all the Christmas cards we had received (which were a great many), get some knitting yarn, and tie all the cards on the tree to fill it in. I think it turned out to be one of the prettiest trees we ever had and a special Christmas.

WARTIME

For an immigrant neighborhood ours was extremely patriotic. I remember parents scolding their children for speaking Italian outside their home because the parents wanted their children to become Americans. They would say that they left the old country behind to find a new life and they expected their children to do everything they could to adapt. When the war started, every window in the flats had an American flag flying. People whose sons were 4-F were embarrassed to the point of saying that their sons had such important jobs vital to the war effort that they had to stay civilians.

I remember Pearl Harbor Day even though I was only eight. We had just come home from church and Daddy had the radio on listening to the news. I was reading the Sunday comics lying on the parlor rug when the regular programming was interrupted to frantic announcements of the attack. We were all stunned and the radio announcers told us all to be aware of our surroundings because no one knew the extent of the attacks that might take place.

Eventually we were all expected to contribute to the war effort. When family members went into the service, small red, white, and blue flags with the appropriate number of stars were hung in windows. We had one star for Frank and one for Mildred since she was an Army nurse. Everyone saved cooking grease and tin cans as well as any other metal. Also, rubber products were saved and eventually picked up by volunteers to be recycled for war materials. We had ration books for food and gas. People could only purchase so much meat, butter, coffee and so on. Anyone who had a car couldn't get gas very often and tires were simply not available. We all learned to manage since we were constantly reminded of the sacrifices and horrible conditions our troops were living in.

Mother became an air raid warden and we had alerts on a regular basis. Since Hoboken's waterfront was part of the port of New York Harbor and many, many ships left from there, it was a target. Our windows had to have shades and curtains that didn't permit light to filter through and when the alerts sounded all external lights had to be extinguished. The air raid wardens would make their rounds and bang on any door that had lights showing. Even cigarettes couldn't be smoked because even that small light could be detected. Of course, I thought all these precautions were really cool and exciting and I liked it when we had an air raid drill. Sometimes we would climb up to the roof of our building and watch everything go dark. I don't imagine Mother or Daddy had a clue that we did that but it was really something to look across the Hudson and see New York City shut down. With Daddy being a police officer he worked a great deal extra. Military ships as well as merchant ships were constantly coming and going out of the harbor.

Everyone tried to do something to help the war effort, from the older people right down to the toddlers. Children were reminded about doing without when they wanted something they couldn't have and the adults sank every extra penny in war savings bonds. We would have bond rallies that became street parties with bands and celebrities up on a platform rousing the crowd to buy, buy, and buy. At school, war savings stamps were sold. A stamp cost a dime and you received a book with spaces to glue in the stamps. When the book was filled, you turned it in for a savings bond, so we were encouraged to save our pennies until we had a dime and then buy our savings stamp.

Nobody understood exactly what a sacrifice it was to save those pennies instead of buying penny candy. There was nowhere that we went that we didn't see posters with ships being sunk and planes being shot down and all the POWs. The radio was filled with war news as well as all the newspapers. When we went to the movies there were the newsreels to remind us and at the end of each and every movie or cartoon or newsreel was the statement reminding us to buy war bonds. We were all very, very gung ho for our GIs and just wanted to do all we could to get them home as early as possible and no sacrifice was too great.

Daddy worked all along the waterfront and along a street that had many industrial plants such as Lipton Tea, American Can, Tootsie Roll, etc. He once actually caught some scumbags bringing in contraband and hiding it in the cellar of a saloon. He was honored for this arrest with a commendation that he received and that is in the police department records.

During the war, Daddy would buy packages of Tootsie Roll candy to send to Frank. The selection wasn't just the Tootsie Rolls, it included chocolate and butterscotch fudge, hard candy, etc. The boxes were five-pound packages and came in sturdy cardboard boxes. Frank loved to get them and so did his buddies. Sometimes Daddy would bring a box home for us and what a treat it was. At Christmastime, these same manufacturers would present Daddy with a special gift of their products, especially Lipton Tea. They included their dried, packaged soups, teas of all kinds, crackers, and other things. These usually went off to Frank as well, but I remember them still coming after the war was over.

Top: Patrick Kennedy and Agnes Kennedy
Bottom: Janet Kennedy, St. Michael's High School senior portrait, 1951

Army Cadet Nurse Mildred Kennedy and
United States Marine Frank Kennedy - World War II

Top: Johhny and Patty Hayes, January 20, 1951 wedding
Bottom: Patty Kennedy working at Rockefeller Center

Top: United States Marine Mick Murphy
Bottom: United Sates Navy WAVE Janet Kennedy

The Kennedy siblings (L to R):
Janet, Patty, Mildred, and Frank

Mildred and Jim Murphy

Front (L-R): Frank, Mildred, Patty, Agnes Kennedy (mom)
Back (L-R): Uncle Dominick, Patrick Kennedy (dad)

Top: Janet Kennedy holding "Mick Jr."
Bottom: Patty Kennedy

The Kennedy Hoboken Trio: (L to R) Janet, Patty and Mildred

CHAPTER 4

HOBOKEN TEENAGERS

AFTER THE WAR

High school was fun and Patty and I went to school together. St. Michael's High School was in Union City, New Jersey, and fairly far from where we lived. There were no school buses in those days and usually we took regular buses. If we were lucky, we had bus tickets to take us from 5th to Clinton Street and 14th to Willow Avenue. Then we took another bus to Union City and from there a short walk to the school. Since we had to change buses during the trip, sometimes we would walk up the viaduct to school because we would be late if we had just missed the second bus. Being late required the students to stay after school for detention and we would get in trouble with Mother if we were late because we had our "work" to do before we went to our paying jobs.

Hoboken is at the foot of the Palisades and just about all the rest of New Jersey is built on the land above the Palisades. It was just a sheer drop from the top of the cliffs down, and a viaduct was constructed to span the area from the lower land to the top of the cliffs. Many a day we had to walk the entire route since the bus tickets had all been used. I guess it was probably three to four miles in all and we really never minded the walk. Some days after school was out we would fool around until we had missed the bus and had to walk home regardless. We usually got in trouble with Mother since we were too late to get our "work" done.

Mildred and Frank had left home years earlier. Mildred had gone to nurses training where she was required to live in the nurses' home until she graduated. After graduating from St. Michael's where he had been a star halfback on the football team, Frank joined the Marine Corps and served for three and a half years during WWII in North Carolina, China, and Japan.

I have to start off by saying that Patty was my best friend as well as my darling sister when I was a teen. We were always together and had the same friends. I don't know how she felt about it but I thought it was great. We were very, very close as kids and until we were separated by circumstances, we remained that way. I feel so blessed that we are near each other again and can visit from time to time. Even though we aren't real twins we were always treated as such and we do have lots of likes and dislikes that we share. Of course, Mildred and Frank were very dear to us but with them being so much older, we didn't always have the opportunity to spend time with them very often.

There was only one Catholic high school in Hoboken and it was an all-girls school, Sacred Heart Academy. It catered to the rich and prominent and snobs. We wouldn't have attended that school if it was free so we had to go to another city to find a Catholic High School.

Mildred and Frank had both attended St. Michael's High School in Union City so naturally Patty and I followed suit. Frank had been a star running back in high school. Our school colors were Kelly green and white with gold trim. We were known as the Fighting Irish and were mascots of Notre Dame. In fact, Frank Leahy, while still coach of Notre Dame, came to the school for a visit and addressed the students as a morale builder. However, we were nothing like our idols since we never had a winning season while I was there or even close to it. We were whipped just about every game. St. Michael's had an attendance of approximately 350-400 students and the surrounding public schools had enrollments in the thousands. We proudly supported our teams and screamed our heads off at all the games, football and basketball, only to go down to defeat most of the time.

Our rival school, St. Cecilia's in Edgewood, had good

teams because they had a great coach – Vince Lombardi, the Hall of Fame Green Bay Packers coach for whom the Super Bowl trophy is named. Vince Lombardi was a member of the Fordham University "Seven Blocks of Granite," as was Mildred's high school history teacher, Ed Franco. The students knew if they wanted to avoid a lesson to ask him a football question. He would spend the rest of the period talking about it.

The one and only time I remember a winning game was when we played St. Peter's Prep. It was a private all-boys school in Jersey City and they were a powerhouse. St. Michael's had just enrolled a senior who was an excellent player and they couldn't wait to get him on the field. The first time he was eligible to play was that game against St. Peter's. We won by a touchdown and kept St. Peter's scoreless. We were out of our minds with pride.

Our stadium was not on our school grounds and it was a bit of a walk back to the campus. It was school custom to have our band march back to the school to have a pep rally after a victory. Since it rarely happened, most of us who attended the game followed the band back. At this time, we had not won any games and to beat St. Peter's was a monumental win. One of the nuns who happened to be there grabbed the baton from the drum major and led the band back to school. I remember watching the movie about Knute Rockne where a nun led the Notre Dame team off the field after a thrilling victory. Maybe that's where our nun got the idea.

We were just ecstatic and made enough noise marching back to make everyone know that we had won. However, the next day we discovered that our new player had been ineligible and our victory was overturned. But it was good while it lasted.

Our basketball teams were better than our football teams and had fairly good stats at times. Pat Finnigan was our basketball coach and was very handsome. Lots of the girls had a crush on him but he was too involved in his team to pay any attention to them. Not too many years ago, my son Michael ran into him during some sort of basketball event that Michael was covering for the Houston Chronicle. Knowing that Pat Finnigan was a Michaelian he mentioned that his mother and aunt had not only graduated from St. Michael's but that we had attended while Pat was still coach. Michael said he was truly tickled to find someone who had actually heard of St. Michael's, much less had actually attended the school. But another reason people knew about St. Michael's was that legendary Boston Celtics player-coach Tommy Heinsohn played for the school while Patty and I went there and also starred in school plays.

St. Michael's was a great school and I thoroughly enjoyed it. It was the top rated school in New Jersey and we were very proud of this distinction. We all got to know most of the kids we went to school with so we had lots of friends. We had to wear uniforms and, of course, they always fit us like bags. Mother always allowed plenty of room for growth. We also had to wear stockings. Nylons were in short supply due to the war and if you were fortunate to find any they were extremely expensive. Mother always bought us cotton hose or something called lisle which was like a heavy rayon. All of these could be mended and lasted forever and we HATED THEM. Some of the dorky kids wore them also and so I guess we joined the group. They were really ugly and so we would camouflage them somewhat by wearing bobby sox over them.

Daddy always bought our shoes and again we always got PRACTICAL shoes, usually OXFORDS: STURDY, WELL-MADE, and UGLY. I was sure no guy would ever consider me as someone he would like to date since I was burdened with the stupidest clothes anyone had ever seen and I was absolutely embarrassed by them. We also COULD NOT wear make-up to school so as soon as we cleared the campus out came the lipstick, etc.

The boys had to wear slacks, dress shirts, ties, and jackets as their uniforms. They hated that as much as we hated our uniforms. Since we didn't have air conditioning in the

74

school, by spring the guys were dying of heat. At times, they were permitted to take their jackets off but the ties remained and the sleeves could not be rolled up.

On Thursday, we had gym. We had ugly, ugly, ugly gym clothes that we had to wear during gym class and we never wanted anyone to see us in those awful things. We had to keep our stockings on and put on navy blue bloomers that came just below the knee and, of course, since they were bloomers they had elastic around the bottom. We had middy blouses to finish off this god-awful outfit and so we cavorted around for an hour until we finished our sentences and were let out. I remember seeing Hitler's youth groups in the newsreels and thinking that's exactly what we all looked like.

As I said earlier, Mother started me in school when I was four, so I was only thirteen when I started high school. I think I was the youngest freshman at that time. Some of my classmates were also thirteen but their birthdays were soon after school started. My birthday didn't come around until close to the end of the school year, so I was considered a baby to a good many of the kids who knew how old I was. Some of my friends were still in grammar school and it was hard for me to fit in. I was very tall, 5'8", so my age wasn't too apparent to some of the others. Patty was shorter and skinny and kids called her Olive Oyl, Popeye's girlfriend in the popular Popeye cartoon.

The freshman classes were held in a building across from the regular high school, so we were isolated from the normal routine. We couldn't wait for our sophomore year so we could move into the other building and make fun of the new freshmen. Meanwhile, Patty was on the main campus involved with the Catholic Action Club, Chemistry Club, French Club, and yearbook.

Our principal was Sister Margaret Veronica, otherwise known as Maggie. Almost all of the nuns had nicknames and they were well aware of it. The worst thing anyone could do was to slip and call them by their nicknames to their faces. I don't think it happened very often but I'm sure the nuns got a kick out of it when we weren't around. The one I remember the most was our biology teacher, Sister Mary Eleanor, who was "the jeep" to all of us. She was a real character and always made me laugh. She usually had her sleeves rolled up to her elbows and could be tough, but we loved her. She made biology so much fun; we never minded her class even when we were dissecting a frog.

Our school was affiliated with St. Michael's Monastery, which was a short walk from the school. It was one of the most beautiful churches we had ever seen, both inside and out. It had a huge dome in the center of the roof and spectacular paintings and mosaics. The monks lived on the premises and were rarely seen. The grounds were resplendent and very serene. They had outdoor, life-sized Stations of the Cross which were open to the public to visit if they chose to do so.

Every year at the beginning of the school year all the students had to make a three-day retreat at the monastery. We sat together as classes and had to hear Mass, pray, and listen to some very boring sermons. We didn't dare whisper to one another, wiggle around, or heaven forbid, laugh, during the services. I don't think I will ever forget the time when I was a senior and we had a priest who had a speech impediment give the sermon. He couldn't pronounce an "R" or an "L" and would say them as a "W." Every time the poor man would say "pway" for pray or "bwace" for brace we would die. We tried everything to cover up the snickering. We pretended that we were coughing, sneezing, etc. The nuns were on to us but they were content to let us hang ourselves. The final one that put us over the edge was when he was very passionately and vehemently stating, "You must follow the parade, the parade, the parade," etc., except it came out as "You must fowwow the pawade, the pawade, the pawade," and by then we were rolling in the aisles. Needless to say, most of us wound up in detention for that day.

Our school population was so small that all of us had to

try out for Glee Club when we were freshmen. Mr. O'Donnell was our music and Glee Club director and he held auditions in the gym. He was very kind to those who couldn't carry a tune and sent them on their way. When it came to my turn to hit a key I told him it was too high for me. This went on until he finally found one that suited me. Since I couldn't carry a tune in a bucket, he suggested that I not harbor any wishes to be a singer, and added that I was the only female he had ever encountered who was a natural bass. I have always wondered about my lack of musical talent, since Mother was a piano player, Daddy was a trumpet player, and Mildred, Frank, and Patty also played the trumpet and I became a DRUM MAJOR. I don't know if they were tired of teaching us to play and just gave up on me since I was the youngest or if I was simply a lost cause. My husband Mick says I have a natural ability to be always flat and off key.

St. Michael's student body was comprised mostly of kids from Hoboken, so we were among friends from the beginning. All of us were bus kids and had to wait on the corner directly down from the school. On this corner was an ice cream and hamburger joint called Steckman's that was absolutely flooded after school. If you have ever seen the TV show "Happy Days" and saw "Arnolds" place then you know exactly what I mean. Lots of times we couldn't even get inside the door much less get served. It was our favorite place to put on our lipstick, take off stockings, and fix our hair.

Noontime was even worse so some of us decided to go to Lindeman's, which was the same sort of place but was never as crowded. Down the street from the school was Lagazio's, another place similar to the first one, but more like a candy store than a hangout. They recognized all the kids who came there and who had older sisters and brothers who had spent time there, so those of us who had siblings who attended Michael's were always welcome.

Styles then were strictly post-war. The "New Look" was in which meant very long shirts and very high collars, almost a Victorian look. The skirts were usually full and swishy. Shoes for the girls were ballerina slippers even to the ribbons tied around the ankle. The boyish bobs and the "DA's" or "Duck Tail" were the hottest things for hairdos. The guys wore pegged pants, flashy ties, and long dangling key chains; almost but not quite like the "Zoot Suits" that were the rage during that period. They wore clodhopper shoes, which seemed to enhance their aura. Their hair was cut close and rarely was over half an inch. The "Crew Cut" was IN and popular.

Dancing was the rage and everybody worked at being good at it. There were dances at most of the Catholic Church halls during the week. Lots of the kids went stag, especially the girls. If you didn't have anyone else to dance with, the girls danced with each other. Since I was so tall I generally had to lead and had to remember that when I danced with a guy I had to let him lead. We danced the "Jitterbug," naturally, as well as the smooth "Peabody," and the lovers' dance, the "Montclair."

Our school had a cafeteria, although they didn't serve food. It was just a place to eat lunches we brought, which was often for us, and pass time before classes resumed. They did have a jukebox down there and lots of us played the music and danced. I know I watched most of the time instead of dancing because all the best dancers (the cool kids) showed off during lunchtime and the rest of us would never compete because we would be laughed off the floor. But it was still fun just to watch.

Our church had dancing on Wednesday evening. Patty, our very best friend Pat Cuddihy, and I went to the hall just about every Wednesday night. Sometimes another girl, Norma Kahl, would go as well. Patty had a crush on Hank Boehm, Pat had crush on Joe Stevens, and I had a crush on Pete Maggarelli. They rarely paid any attention to us and usually didn't ask us to dance. We were thrilled when they would bother with us, and while I'm sure we thought we were being cool and sort of ignoring them, I'm just as sure we were wearing our hearts on our sleeves and these guys were well aware of it and were having a ball at our expense.

Our Lady of Grace also had a drum and bugle marching band and they were wonderful. They won many awards and we were so very proud of them. We girls always went to the parades they marched in, and believe me; parades in those days were often, as they still are. Brother Frank was in several drum and bugle bands after he came home from the war and even after he married. Most of the bands he was a member of went into local competitions and then on to national competitions and won almost every one. His bands marched in the most prestigious parades, notably the Rose Bowl, and always received an overwhelming ovation. It is still a very popular pastime back east.

Anyway, Hank, Joe, and Pete were members of our band so we always had to be there to cheer them on. Some of the parades were in other cities so it meant taking buses to get there and then usually having to walk distances to get to the parade route, but we never seemed to mind. Afterwards the bands would go back to the bus areas and so would we. We would all mingle and yak it up. Since these guys were always really pumped up after a parade and since we knew everyone in the band we all enjoyed it. Sometimes Mother would go with the band in the buses since she was the one who designed the new band uniforms, which were very sharp, and also selected the material for them, so she went occasionally to take care of any problems that were encountered with the uniforms. Eventually, Hank asked Patty out, Joe and Pat became an item, and Pete also asked me out. I guess perseverance is always worthwhile.

Patty, Pat, and I were all committee members of the church's Catholic Youth Organization and we were responsible for coming up with ideas to present to the priests for CYO activities. One of our younger priests, Father Brennan, came up with an idea for a little theater group comprised of members of the CYO.

Father Brennan was born in the good old USA, but was raised by two maiden aunts who came from the Old Sod

(Britain, the old country) and had heavy brogues. He picked up the brogue as a child and never lost it, so most people thought he too came from Ireland. He was very conservative and could be full of fire and brimstone when he preached or encountered any deviation from church teaching.

I remember one Easter Sunday when he was in the pulpit giving the sermon. Our pulpit was very high over the congregation and serviced by a spiral staircase, therefore the priests literally looked down on the people beneath them. Some poor woman who happened to be directly in his line of vision had all her Easter finery on including a very lovely hat, which was round with lots of tulle and flowers on it, but lacking a crown, which left the top of her head exposed. He went berserk and pointed her out to each and every one of us for defying the church by not having her head covered. I'm sure she was humiliated and wished she could have crawled under her seat but he never let up on her and used her as an example to all of us females, not only about head coverings but about being bold, daring, and insolent in God's house.

However, with all of us young people he was wonderful. We thought the world of him. He became our mentor as well as our priest. He made our theater group a wonderful outlet for us and we became very successful as actors, backstage hands, cue cards holders, ushers, ticket takers, and organizers. We put on a variety of plays, starting with an old-fashioned melodrama with the evil villain and the pure and beautiful maiden. There was a part for an Indian girl in the play and since I had very long and very black hair I was selected to play that part. My entire dialogue consisted of saying "Ugh" whenever someone spoke to me. I was thirteen years old and the acting bug bit me. I think Patty was in this play also and I know she had a better part than I did; any of that cast had a better part than I did. I remember Mildred was in the audience and I could hear her laughing. Her laugh was very contagious and I had a hard time controlling myself, but we made it through and we had a great reception from the audience, with lots of applause and cheers.

I don't remember which play it was that Patty played a maid à la Zazoo Pitts. I'm pretty sure you don't have a clue as to who she was, but she was a great Hollywood actress who was always cast as a flighty, silly, dumb soul with a heart of gold. Patty was so good that she stole the show and got a great hand as the cast took their bows.

I wasn't considered for a role in that play, and since I played the unimportant role of the Indian in the first play, I was constantly overlooked after that as a not-so-good actress. My first big break came when we were doing Best Foot Forward, which is a Broadway play later made into a movie, and also the movie where Lucille Ball and Desi Arnaz met. The plot is the one where a famous Hollywood actress goes to a military academy prom as a publicity stunt. She has a tough publicity agent, a guy nobody likes.

The fellow who had been originally cast in that role had to drop out and Father Brennan asked me to read the part until he could get a replacement. Since I was only reading for the interim, I never put any effort into the rehearsals. Well, to make a long story short, they never could come up with a substitute and I wound up doing the part. I don't think anyone had any confidence that I would perform well, including Mother who insisted that I quit. I was even more determined to show everyone that I COULD DO IT. I guess I did okay because at the finale I was called back to take an extra bow and Father Brennan actually hugged me and said I had done an extra good job. I was only fourteen at the time and that sure boosted my ego. We did a number of plays but eventually the members of the group started leaving to pursue other endeavors and the little theater was no more.

When Patty and I reached the ripe old age of fourteen we had to get jobs. Since Patty was older she was the first to go to work. She started at Fisher and Biers, a huge "five and dime" store. She worked right after school let out to early evening and then came home to eat, help with the dishes, and then do homework. On Saturdays, she worked all day long until the store closed at 8 PM.

Saturday was payday and when the store closed at night, Patty received a small brown envelope that contained cash. Mother was always waiting outside the store when it closed so that she could take the earnings. Patty might then receive a twenty-five cent allowance for spending money.

Patty was an obedient daughter and the family peacemaker, so she would turn the money over without complaining. Mother always called me "her baby" even long after I became an adult and had adult children. But I still challenged her growing up, although not as much as Mildred did. Mildred and Mother had some intense and memorable disagreements. While Mildred and I might challenge Mother, Patty never did. The rest of us thought she was the favorite child but we also understood it was for good reason because she was so forgiving, unselfish, and loving.

I also started at Fisher and Biers when I was fourteen and by then Patty had moved on to another job. Since we didn't know anyone who worked at Fisher and Biers who lived in our area, both Patty and I always had to walk to and from the store alone when we worked there. There were no buses that covered the route we would take. In the winter, it was not only cold but very dark and we always took a short cut through the park to get home. I wouldn't do that now for all the tea in China but I guess we didn't think anything of it back then.

I worked at the cosmetics counter and it was the same scenario as with Patty. When I first started working, I made 35 cents an hour and after almost three years I was getting 50 cents an hour. I worked and then gave my pay envelope to Mother and received my 25 cent or so allowance for the week. We wouldn't have minded if the money was needed for the family, but we had never had any problems like that, ever. I'm not saying things were always easy but we always managed. The problem wasn't need, it was greed.

Our weekends were never ours. If we were working outside the house we still had "our work" to do at home. We also did ninety percent of the cooking and grocery shopping. Dishes were mandatory every night and usually after school we would get home, do our "work," then run to the stores, come home, prepare dinner, eat, do the dishes, and then homework. Saturdays we cleaned the house from top to bottom every single week. We couldn't go out with our friends even to go to the beach or a movie. The work came first. Sundays we were allowed to sleep late because we went to twelve o'clock mass. When we got home, we had to cook dinner, which was always a big meal since it was Sunday. Sometimes we would have stuffed chickens with all the works and by the time we finished with the dishes it was usually around five. We could go out with our girlfriends then, take a walk, and get some ice cream. It was not too much to look forward to.

What was fun to look forward to was "cruising" on weekends. Most of the kids cruised Washington St. but not by car. We all walked, the guys going one way and the girls going the other way. We would stop in Schoening's for a sundae and sometimes others would join us. Schoening's was THE place to meet up and it was larger than most of the other ice cream places and had the best jukebox. We spent many an evening there.

We were allowed to have boyfriends when we were sixteen but at first Patty wasn't permitted to go on a date with just the guy. Mother insisted that I had to go along. This didn't last long but I know that it was humiliating for her to drag her kid sister along. The first boy who I remembered asking Patty out was Bobby Mercer. His buddy was Joe Nolan, who became my date. Joe was a nice guy, but I was already 5'9" and he was maybe 5'4" tall. He was skinny and had a flat face that seemed to have had a steamroller run over it. Anyway, I was mortified to be seen with him.

Patty's romance with Bobby didn't last very long but Joe seemed to have a passion for me. He sent me heart-shaped boxes of candy, flowers, and many other loving offerings but I was mean enough to send most of it back to him; I just wanted to be left alone and find a guy on my own. Eventually he gave up. I wasn't very nice to him, as I realize now, but I was just uncomfortable with him especially without Patty there to back me up.

Patty at one time had been friends with a boy named Albert. One night he came to the house to take Patty out and Mother answered the door said, "Hi Albert. Did you know you and Patty are cousins?" Patty had been dating our cousin!

We both had our share of beaus, which meant maybe a movie and walking home holding hands. We said goodnight on the stoop and no kissing was considered until we were going steady. Sometimes a date consisted of taking a walk and stopping for ice cream and walking home again. How innocent it all was then. We had heard about drugs but never knew anyone who was involved with them.

Sex was strictly verboten and none of us would even consider anything like that. Believe it or not, a good many of the girls didn't have a clue as to the mechanics of sex. I remember girls who got pregnant while in school. It was a horror story for their families and the girls were shipped off to relatives until after the baby was born. The baby was always adopted and the shame and the disgrace the family was submitted to was awful. All the tongues wagged and the gossips had a field day. The family never disclosed any information and simply said their daughter was ill and sent to an institution for care. Many times the girls never returned to their homes because their parents didn't want them to live there again. Thank God, we as a society are more compassionate now and handle it differently and in better and nicer ways.

CHAPTER 5

LEAVING HOBOKEN

Mildred and Jim Murphy

Hoboken remains a foundational and nostalgic part of our lives, especially after we all married and moved away. We three Kennedy sisters often joke that we had to marry Irishmen to get out of Hoboken ... and two of us married Murphys! Patty's husband Johnny jokes that we Kennedy sisters found "unsuspecting" Irishmen!

Mildred met the love of her life, James Patrick Murphy, at the end of World War II in 1945 while she served as a nurse in the US Army Nurse Corps. However, there was quite a journey before that would happen.

She graduated from St. Michael's High School in 1941 and then in 1942 began nursing training at St. Mary's Hospital in Hoboken and became a Registered Nurse. In 1944, she joined the newly created Army Corps as a Cadet Nurse and went through a four-week training course.

She was on her way to serve in Tuscaloosa, Alabama when they asked for volunteers to work at Halloran Army Hospital in Willowbrock, Staten Island. World War II was the largest and most violent war in all of history, with seemingly endless casualties. The Army transformed an existing facility into the largest Army hospital in the world. There they housed thousands of very, very badly wounded soldiers as ships came in to New York Harbor from the war. That site was chosen as a debarkation hospital so that the wounded would be close to the piers and docks and could be transported to Halloran as soon as possible.

Not every nurse could deal with the intense reality of Halloran. Mildred volunteered because she knew she had the training and could handle it emotionally. There were seventy-three nurses at Halloran. Initially, each met with a psychiatrist to prepare them for the horrific and gruesome injuries they would see. They were told to not show their emotions until they got off the floor. Mildred was deeply affected by what she saw but wouldn't show it.

Halloran had the Army's best neurosurgeons and orthopedic specialists. The soldiers were so seriously injured that they had to be treated for months at Halloran before they could be sent to a hospital nearer to their homes. It was an impressive facility with gates guarded by military police (MPs) as well as numerous barracks to house patients and military and medical personnel.

Ships arrived in New York carrying 5-10,000 wounded soldiers at a time. "52s," military ambulances like those shown in the MASH movie and TV show, would go in convoys to the piers through Bayonne. Police would block off the streets in New York leading to the docks so they could go up on the ships. They would go back and forth all day long and transport up to 10,000 wounded soldiers to Halloran. Many times, as fellows would come down on stretchers, they would touch the ground of the pier and start crying because they were home. The Red Cross Grey Ladies would be there and the first thing they would do is give these fellows a cigarette to calm their nerves down. That shocks us now but that is what they did back then.

Many of the wounded came from the Battle of the Bulge, aka the Battle of Ardennes. This was a major battle fought in northern France during WWII that began on December 16, 1944 and ended on January 25, 1945. It was a last ditch surprise offensive launched by Hitler during the deadly cold winter of 1944 in which 250,000 German troops were sent across an eighty-five-mile stretch of the Allied front, from southern Belgium into Luxembourg. The German troops advanced some fifty miles into the Allied lines, along a seventy-mile front, creating a deadly "bulge" pushing into Allied defenses. Eventually the Allies regained the lost land but about 21,000 American soldiers were killed and 43,000 injured in the intense fighting.

They came from other battles as well. Halloran housed thirty men who had no arms and no legs. Some were blind while others might have been missing an ear. Many required surgery to put plates in the back of their skulls where it had been blown off. Mildred was in the operating room for four months straight all day long assisting with those surgeries.

The Japanese had tortured countless soldiers. For instance, if they didn't bow a certain way the Japanese would take machetes and cut off their ears, arms, legs, anything. They would blind them - just do terrible things to them. By contrast, German POWs held by the US were treated so well at Halloran that those POWs didn't want to go back home to Germany. The German POWs helped in the operating room, worked on the floors, and did a lot of cooking. It was a striking contrast to how the Japanese treated our POWs.

Captain Croce was the top surgeon and, while difficult to work with, did wonderful work in the operating room. Mildred worked alongside of him, putting plates in the backs of skulls and other intense surgeries. They spent from 7 AM to 5 PM every day for four months working on these patients. They worked with a wiring that had to be just perfect to heal each nerve. It was tedious work and it took hours and hours, putting metal plates in the back of the skull. They worked on paraplegics and did everything they could to restore some comfort and use of their arms, since they were basically paralyzed from the waist down. They just needed so much care but Captain Croce did unbelievable work in the operating room. The only nourishment they received was a little orange juice through a straw through their mask. Mildred admired him and still thinks about him often. He was a great, great doctor.

The nurses had to do almost everything for these young guys and it was pretty difficult. It was hard at times for Mildred to see them suffer so much since so many were only nineteen-twenty years old and the same age as many of the nurses. The hospital really focused on keeping the patients' morale up and their minds off their difficult circumstances. Big entertainers like Bob Hope, Frank Sinatra, and Jerry Colonna would come to the hospital's big Red Cross auditorium and they did a fabulous job entertaining them. It was the era of the Big Band and so there were some great concerts too. They went to great lengths to get the men to laugh and to keep their minds off the difficult circumstances. Mildred remembers one day Bob Hope went up to a patient to shake his hand but the young man didn't have any arms. Hope turned around with tears in his eyes and he felt so terrible about it.

Bob Hope was so gracious and wonderful. One evening before a show, he was talking to the patients and saw a young patient sitting by himself in a corner of the auditorium. He said to him, "What are you doing way over there? Come over and sit right here." Hope brought him over to the front row and told him to sit in a seat in the middle. Well, that seat was the General's seat and he had not yet arrived.

Nurses were only allowed to see the shows if they took a patient there with them so Mildred was there that night. She and the others all thought "Oh my goodness, he is in the General's seat!" As General DeVoe walked in, all those who could stood and saluted him as they tried not to laugh. The General made a sharp left hand turn to his seat and saw the young patient sitting there. By now all the patients were crying from laughing so hard. The General shook the patient's hand and everyone had a really enjoyable night together.

One of the toughest cases for her was a soldier who was so badly hurt at the Battle of the Bulge they put him in a private room and called for his parents. They finally arrived and as the elevator opened for them to walk down the hall to his private room, the soldier died in Mildred's arms. It was very sad.

But there were good stories as well. Sergeant Hoffman was a twenty-year-old paratrooper who had been injured badly at the Battle of the Bulge. He was being taken into the operating room to amputate to his left leg (he had already lost one arm).

Katherine Cornell, "the First Lady of the theatre" was performing for the patients there. She saw Sergeant Hoffman, signed a $10 bill, and gave it to him. She told him, "Always keep this with you." A year or two later, she again performed at Halloran for the patients. Sgt. Hoffman was still there recuperating and he asked Mildred to wheel him to the show. After the show, he asked to be wheeled to her dressing room. When she came out of her dressing room, he waved his $10 bill. She saw him and said "Oh my goodness. It is Sergeant Hoffman!" She walked up to him, gave him a big hug and kiss, and broke down.

Katherine asked if she could wheel Sgt. Hoffman back to the hospital ward, and Mildred said she would be very honored if she would do that, so Katherine wheeled him back to the ward. At first she backed away when she saw the patients but then said "I have to do this." Mildred told her to do whatever she needed to but that it was OK if she didn't. Well she went off to the ward and visited many of the patients. She had tears in her eyes when she realized the ordeal they were facing but she was wonderful with them. When she was done, she broke down as they took her back to the tour bus. She kept in touch with Mildred after that. She wrote a letter saying how wonderful the nurses all were to her and that she would never forget what she saw in the ward. Mildred has been told those letters are worth a lot of money because of the fame of Katherine Cornell, but she vowed to keep them forever and she has.

Then there was Sergeant Wallace, a twenty-year-old paratrooper who was machine-gunned badly at the Battle of the Bulge. He was put in the corner of one room in what they called a striker frame, a type of bed where he could be turned over and brought back upright so he wouldn't get a harmful bedsore. He suffered greatly and was in very bad shape. He never laughed or smiled. He would often sing lyrics from the 1945-jump blues song "Caledonia" by Louis Jordan and the Tympany Five.

The first stanza is "Caledonia, Caledonia, what makes your big head so hard?" The second stanza is "I love her; I love her just the same." But instead of singing the second stanza he would squeeze his arms together in pain and say "Rocks!" This is how he expressed the pain he constantly felt.

The Women's Army Corps (WACs) was on base and they had their own softball team. Captain Garraghan asked the nurses if they could form their own team to play them. They wanted entertainment at all times so these fellas were never left to be thinking about things. They had a couple of practices, and Mildred got ready to play. The nurses got off their floor, put their uniforms on, and went out to play. They thought there would only be a few people there but to their astonishment, the place was packed! Mildred thought, "Oh my gosh, where did all of these people come from?" Included among the many patients out there was Sergeant Wallace on his striker frame, leaning on his stomach and looking up.

The WACs were big women and the nurses were little peanuts like Mildred. They scored something like nineteen runs in the first half of the inning. Mildred was third to bat in the bottom of the inning and she thought, "All I have to do is swing the bat three times and sit down." Somehow, she swung really hard and hit the ball. She swung so hard that she spun around. Everyone started yelling, "Run!" So Mildred excitedly started running and then everyone started yelling even more. She thought, "Wow, I must have done something great!" But then she realized she was running to THIRD base!! Now everyone was yelling to run to FIRST base so Mildred ran between the catcher and the pitcher to first base.

Mildred had such big feet that her patients called her "Feet." Sure enough, she tripped over those big feet and went face first into first base.

At the end of the game, it was like forty to nothing. The

nurses were all sitting on the bench when the top surgeon, Captain Croce, came marching across the field towards their dugout looking right at Mildred. He was a very strict man but with the nature of his job, he had to be. Mildred was thinking, "Oh my gosh, I'm in deep trouble" as he walked directly to her and said, "Kennedy, stand up right now." She stood, expecting to be scolded. He said, "Kennedy, I want you to know that you did something that none of us could ever do. You made Sergeant Wallace laugh. You made him laugh so hard he started crying because of the mistake you made." Mildred smiled and said, "Captain I'm so happy I did that." And she truly was happy!

Mildred was supposed to go to the war in the Pacific in September 1945, but thankfully, the war ended in August. The Surgeon General decided everyone needed to stay in the United States and treat all the wounded returning home at the end of the war. She was at Halloran on VE Day and VJ Day. They stayed as long as they were needed. In December 1945, they left and returned to civilian life.

Mildred and the other nurses who started at Halloran served for almost a year at Halloran. There were times when working in the hospital was wonderful as they helped the patients and saved many lives. There were other times that were extremely difficult as the soldiers crying and moaning made them sad, and when lives couldn't be saved despite their best efforts. But overall it was a wonderful experience for Mildred.

Mother told me that when Mildred left the service, she cried because she didn't want to leave the soldiers. It was very satisfying to her and something she felt she had to do. Mildred was truly happy there. They made it a point to makes things fun and happy for the patients and to keep their morale up. They also tried to make the patients laugh. For example, Mildred would fill a syringe up with tomato juice and then pretend she was drinking blood out of it. The patients made the nurses laugh too. Laughter was truly good medicine for the patients and the nurses.

Mildred and the other nurses showed a great deal of skill, patience, love, and tender care to these wounded heroes. Many others and I greatly admire her and her fellow nurses for that.

Jim Murphy

Jim's parents, James A. Murphy and Anne Tracey, met on a ship coming from Ireland. Anne was from Galway and James was from Belfast. James was married previously and had four children, but then his first wife died. He didn't tell Anne about the four children until they were married!

James and Anne had two sons together, Bill and Jim. Bill was an All-State halfback at Kearney High School. He had scholarship offers for football but instead enlisted in the Marine Corps. Jim was a Boy Scout and an avid tennis player. The Irish immigrant family had very little money. Everything they had was secondhand. At age seventeen, he enlisted in the Marine Corps. He lied to his mother, saying that the paperwork was to attend West Point, so she signed the papers and off he went to the Marines.

Rumor has it that Mildred met the love of her life, Jim Murphy, while she was his nurse at Halloran but that was not the case. Mildred actually met Jim at a USO dance at the Arcadia Ballroom in New York City. Nurses took patients who were able to get up and around to USO events like this one. If a patient had an 82nd or "Screaming Eagles" 101st Airborne Division patch on their clothing he was like royalty. Both units fought heroically at the Normandy D-Day invasion and at the Bulge.

Jim was there dancing and when he saw Mildred, he asked her to dance. It was love at first sight! Mildred was drawn to this handsome, gentle, and kind man, especially as he looked so sharp. His Dress Blues included many medals, including two Iwo Jima combat medals and the Purple Heart.

When they were dating, Mildred really enjoyed being with him when he dressed in his 4th Division Marine uniform. Even his own family and friends looked with awe at him in his Dress Blues and those medals. But Jim didn't enjoy wearing his Dress Blues and sporting the medals. When he returned from the war, he wanted to forget all the terrible things he witnessed and certainly didn't feel like a hero. He actually let his friends wear his Dress Blues a couple of times in exchange for the use of a car so he could take Mildred on dates to New York City.

Those medals were hard-earned though. Jim was among the Marines to land on the island of Iwo Jima on February 19, 1945, the day of the initial invasion. Iwo Jima was another of the difficult island-hopping campaigns to take back tiny islands in the Pacific from the Japanese. Some of the bloodiest fighting in all of World War II took place on this mostly volcanic island 750 miles from Japan. The ultimate goal was to use Iwo Jima and its three airfields as a staging facility for a potential invasion of mainland Japan. Eventually all but 200 or so of the 21,000 Japanese forces on Iwo Jima were killed, as were almost 7,000 Marines. It remains one of the bloodiest battles in U.S. history.

He was barely eighteen years old when he landed on Iwo Jima as a Marine PFC (private first-class), making about $50 a month. He was a member of the 4th Marine Reserves, the "Fighting Fourth," activated to fight in the Pacific. As the amphibious Higgins LCVP landing craft approached the volcanic beach, he was combing his hair when a US fighter plane flew over his landing craft and headed towards the beach. One of his buddies, who was in his mid-20s and married, kept saying he wasn't going to make it. Jim kept telling him he would be fine. In reality, Jim was too green and naive to know what he was about to face. Within minutes of hitting the beach, his buddy was killed by artillery fire and died instantly, one of 2,400 killed that first day. When President Roosevelt heard the causality reports, he reportedly gasped for the first time since Pearl Harbor. It was a quick awakening for Jim. Most members of his 4th Marine Division would be wiped out during the thirty-five--day fighting on Iwo Jima before the iconic photo was taken of the Marines raising the American flag.

Jim was almost one of those killed on Iwo. The 4th Marine Division was given the task of taking the airfield on Iwo. It was a protracted battle on a sulfurous island with no soil. The Marines couldn't dig in anywhere to seek cover, which is a big reason there were so many casualties. In addition, the Japanese had been entrenched there for twenty years and they were going to fight to the death rather than surrender. They wanted to take as many Marines with them as they could. The 21,000 Japanese soldiers would have to be killed nearly one at a time.

On March 8, 1945, the Marines were under a Japanese mortar barrage and sniper assaults. Jim and another Murphy, good friend Don from Flanders, New Jersey, were with their platoon in a foxhole on the ash-like volcanic island. Jim jumped out of the hole and quickly led an assault advance firing a Browning Automatic Rifle (BAR) in a tactic known as walking fire. It was his job to fire into holes and caves and take out Japanese soldiers.

In a split second, five of Jim's fellow Marines were killed, shot in the jugular by Japanese sharpshooters. Jim was also shot. A bullet hit him in the neck, just missing his jugular vein by a hair but it clipped his vertebrae. Bullets pierced his spine and blew out his shoulder. He remembers, "I guess I put my head up. I don't recall. The next thing I knew I felt a projectile going through my neck and out my back." While two medical corpsman rushed to his aid, his friend Don gave some words of encouragement before being ordered out of the foxhole.

The two medics were then shot and killed and their bodies fell on top of Jim. A courageous fellow Marine jumped out of the hole to tell his commanding officer that there was a live Marine beneath those two bodies. After he was rescued, he was moved to the beach where they were doing triage on the many casualties.

By the grace of God he survived. The hospital ships were overloaded with so many injured that he was transported by a DC3 plane from Iwo. He was flown to Guam, where the hospital was vulnerable to shots from fanatical Japanese strays in the woods. He recalls, "They placed me at the end of a tent and I very vividly recall hearing the doctors saying, 'Don't worry about this kid here. He is not going to live through the morning anyway.'"

His ordeal continued when a converted C 47 cargo plane flying stretcher cases to Pearl Harbor was strafed by enemy machine gun fire and forced to land on Johnson Island, 300 miles west of Hawaii.

Rescued by plane from the island, Jim arrived later in San Francisco and slowly recuperated at Navy hospitals in Corvallis and Eugene, Oregon. Jim loved Oregon, and if it had not been for the fact that he had family in New Jersey, he might have stayed there. The last leg of his recovery was at Portsmouth Naval Hospital in Virginia before receiving a medical discharge six months later.

For Jim, those six months, while he was unaware if his friend Don Murphy had survived, were a nightmare, caused by both the Japanese and the wound, which had paralyzed him from the waist down. During his arduous six-month recovery, Jim was subjected to intense pain from the wound, which exposed sensitive nerves in his hands and arms. However, because the bullet did not sever his spinal cord, he thankfully eventually regained the use of his limbs.

He was fully discharged and in his 4th Marine Division uniform when Mildred met him at the USO. That 4th Marine patch he wore was very important. Famous heavyweight boxing champion Jack Dempsey had a restaurant in New York on Broadway. If you were a veteran from the 101st or the 82nd Airborne or the 4th Marine Division, you were welcome at his restaurant and the drinks were on him.

After the war, Jim attended Seton Hall University on the new GI Bill. He had a big vocabulary and loved the English language, so he got his degree in English. Mildred and Jim enjoyed going to the charming village there in South Orange with its pubs and restaurants. Many veterans would talk about their time in the service but Jim never mentioned that he was in the Marines. He said it wasn't important to talk about it, so he kept everything inside of himself.

Mildred and Jim were married on December 28, 1946, and their son Jimmy was born on July 16, 1948. After Mildred and Jim got married, Patty and I were considered the natural babysitters for our nephew. We loved going to their home because it got us out of our house, but we also really enjoyed our new nephew.

People said World War II veterans never cried. During the Depression, mothers told their sons "Boys don't cry." As a result, many kept everything to themselves and they suffered a great deal because they never talked about their experiences. We now recognize that Jim and others probably had Post Traumatic Stress Disorder (PTSD). But at the time, they treated veterans physically and discharged them without much understanding of or regard for their mental and emotional state.

Jim really struggled through the 1950s into early 60s. He worked in the insurance business for a period of time and bounced from job to job for a few years. They moved at least ten times. Jim would even disappear for a period of time, but he would always return. It was hardest on Jimmy because he was the oldest of five children and it wasn't a stable environment for him in the early years of his life. And of course it was hard on Mildred, but she stayed committed to Jim and the family and continued to be an excellent nurse.

Things gradually got better for Jim and thus the family. For a while, he did some long-term substitute teaching at South Plainfield High School. On one occasion, a tough kid was giving Jim a hard time in class and said, "Hey, Mr. Murphy, what would you do if I put a knife in your face?" Jim responded in a very calm voice, "Well son, the last person that did that was a Jap on Iwo Jima and I slit his throat from one side to another." That kid was shocked but impressed and from then on Jim had strong credibility among those tough teenage boys.

After he got his degree, he thought about going to law school to be an attorney, but with a wife and more children after Jimmy, it wasn't possible. He would later regret not going. Things improved dramatically when Jim and Mildred moved to Westfield, New Jersey in 1969. They bought a nice colonial style home in a great town. Jim taught for fifteen years at Holy Cross High School in Harrison from 8 AM-3 PM and then worked at Diamond Shamrock Chemical Company in Harrison as a chemist from 3:30 -11:30 PM. The students loved him and he was the favorite teacher of many kids at Holy Cross. He would take some of the boys that didn't have dads in their lives to football games. At the school science fair, kids looked for Jim to show him their projects. The nuns loved him and appreciated what a fine and committed teacher he was. His youngest son, Sean, became a teacher and outstanding football coach because he watched the impact his father had on his students and wanted to be like him.

It was a demanding work schedule but the family shared some really good times. The youngest children, Regina and Sean, would stay up until midnight in the TV room for Jim to get home from work. Jim would come home, hang out in the kitchen with Mildred, and watch "The Tonight Show Starring Johnny Carson" while drinking a Miller beer and having a cigarette. Jim and Mildred would spend about an hour just talking and laughing as they watched the show. It was always comforting for Sean and Regina to hear the sound of two beer cans popping open along with laughter in the kitchen.

Jimmy was raised with instability and still grew to be a wonderful person, perhaps in large part because of his relationship with Daddy. But the younger children felt safe, supported, and comforted by the fact that he and Mildred were in a strong and committed relationship and were there for them. They felt he was the sweetest, kindest, most loving dad ever. The Murphy home became a hangout for high school students because of Jim and Mildred. Some of those kids wished they had a dad like Jim.

On the 50th anniversary of Iwo Jima, he was invited to the Larry King Studio to speak on a CNN special about Iwo Jima. He was both proud and sad to tell his story. Even though Mildred had been married to him for almost fifty years, she and her kids were shocked at some of the things that came out. They learned for the first time that he was the point man of a platoon with a BAR semi-automatic rifle and he had many bad and intense experiences. He wasn't too happy about what he had to do but followed orders. He was a very gentle and kind person who wouldn't swat a fly. It was his job to go into the caves where the Japanese soldiers had been living for twenty years. He had to do a lot of terrible but necessary killing.

In the studio, Mildred heard him say, "It was absolutely horrendous. The carnage was brutal." Jim could be emotional, especially at family weddings and the births of grandchildren, but the emotions associated with WWII were not expressed and it took a toll on him. All those previous years he kept all that inside. Prior to the CNN interview, he had never talked about it and wanted to forget about it if he could. As years went on, he developed stomach problems, high blood pressure, and a heart condition. Mildred believed it was because he wouldn't talk about the war. Later in life, he had flashbacks and would wake up thrashing. He felt really badly and was concerned that he might hurt Mildred. That was the case with many World War II veterans.

But returning veterans like Jim also didn't talk about the war because they were so focused on putting their lives together: finding a job, finding a girl or reacquainting with the one they already had, getting married and raising a family, and working for forty to fifty years. Jim learned to do all of that as Mildred devotedly stayed by his side.

In a recent television interview, Mildred said this about

the other WWII vets: "They were very proud to serve their country. When they went into the service some were excited because they were going to finally get a new pair of shoes for the first time ever. Many grew up in a time where none of us had a lot. Maybe you got to eat something and maybe you didn't. We wore hand-me-down clothes. But somehow it was a group of people that went to war and were proud to serve. There was no negative reporting. Everybody was together. They came back, proud to serve their country, and did everything they could to put the country back together again."

Happily, his good buddy from Iwo, Don Murphy, was one of those who made it back. In 1978, Jim and Don found each other and Don attended the wedding of Jim and Mildred's youngest daughter, Regina. It was a happy and joyous reunion of old friends after so much uncertainty. Don had come through the war "without a scratch" and was thankful that Jim, who he feared had died, was well.

Jim had a message for the youth of our country when he finally spoke of his experiences at other 50th anniversary events. He told students to value the freedom that so many servicemen died to safeguard. He said, "Hold it dearly, children. As you go through life, please understand that God blessed you if we were born in this country."

Patty and Johnny

John A. Hayes III ("Johnny") was born on December 7, 1925. His parents were John A. Hayes, Jr. and Katherine Joyce. John Jr. was a three-time NCAA bantamweight boxing champion at the US Naval Academy (Class of 1924) and boxing coach at the 1924 Paris Olympics. She was the revered leader among her eight siblings, and she went on to be a favored schoolteacher. He called her "Kitty" and she called him "Angel Boy" and "Snooks" (after the cartoon character of that name).

They had a strong romance that became a part of US Naval Academy folklore. At the main Naval Academy dress parade, John's Fifth Company won the annual competition for the honor of carrying the colors for the next academic semester. John, as the successful cadet lieutenant and company commander of his unit, received the national and regimental colors. By tradition, the colors were presented by the "O.A.O" (One and Only) of the recipient. So as "Color Girl" Miss Joyce advanced on the arm of Superintendent Wilson, some of John's comrades called out "Kiss her!" This was not part of the tradition, but he wouldn't miss any opportunity to show off his Katherine - so kiss her he did! Some in the large crowd say he lost no time in going through the osculation and that the kiss lingered. It was reported afterwards that Admiral Wilson was about to call "break" but John stopped right before that. For quite a few years afterwards though, this tradition ended after Angel Boy's passionate kiss of his Kitty. It is a well-remembered romance story that remained talked about for years at the Naval Academy.

John and Katherine soon married on November 29, 1924 at Saint Philip and James Catholic Church in Baltimore, and within a year, she was pregnant. Their romantic story ended sadly and tragically when twenty-seven-year-old Katherine died twelve days after giving birth to Johnny. With today's medical advances, she would have survived. She is buried at the Naval Academy, a rare honor for a civilian.

John was grief stricken over the loss of his beloved wife. Although he loved his baby son (Johnny was called Baby Snooks when he was little but the name didn't stick), the pain of losing his cherished wife was overwhelming. His responsibilities as a lieutenant and later captain in the Navy also made it difficult for him to be a parent to Johnny. So Johnny's grandmother, grandfather "Pops," and his loving Uncle Harold raised him. Little Johnny would essentially be raised without his birth mother and father.

Uncle Harold was as gentle, kind, considerate, and loving of a person as you could ever meet. He loved and treated Johnny as if he was his own son. Harold worked as an accountant at Gibson Cox, a designer of naval ships.

He would eventually work the floor on Wall Street because he was so quick and brilliant with numbers. He was known to be a natural athlete and excelled at bowling and playing baseball.

In 1931-34, Johnny's dad was stationed in Shanghai as a lieutenant colonel, serving the high honor of being Chief Engineer over all U.S. Naval ships in China. Despite making only $75 a week, John enjoyed staying in a luxurious hotel with all the amenities he needed.

While in China, John served as a boxing sparring partner for Navy boxers and was often punch drunk from getting hit so hard. A tough little guy at 5'6" and 120 pounds, he was lightning quick and was known, even to the Chinese, for being able to dish it out, too. The first time he tried to leave the ship down the runway, some Chinese men tried to physically stop him. So he did what he knew best - he grabbed them and threw them overboard! He had no problems leaving the ship after that. Another time when he was training Navy boxers, a Marine challenged him to a fight. John wasn't to be messed with, so he put brass knuckles in his gloves, and the Marine soon regretted challenging him.

Johnny's dad married his second wife, Ruth Wickersham, on March 10, 1928 and they had two children, Michael and Patsy. Ruth lived with John in China where she developed a liver disease, which she never really recovered from. She wasn't one to take good care of herself, and she had a habit of drinking too much, to the point where if guys in the Navy wanted to drink, they would find her and have drinks with her. Her new husband also had a drinking problem though, and it hampered their lives, eventually leading to her death at age sixty-three in 1963. Johnny felt his dad accomplished so much up until the end of WWII that he never fully felt the same fulfillment.

From 1934-36, John returned to Philadelphia to work at the Naval Boiler and Turban Lab. The Navy downsized in 1936, so he temporarily left the Navy and took a job at Todd Shipyards. In September 1940, the Navy established the

Navy Bureau of Ships in Washington, DC. The head of the Bureau of Ships was Admiral Edward Cochrane who later became the president of MIT. John was asked to come back to the Navy, where he became head of the boiler section and was promoted to captain. Admiral Hyman Rickover, one of the most famous leaders of World War II, was head of the electrical section. Admiral Cochrane and Captain Hayes were the only two to be awarded the prestigious Legion of Merit medal. John also received the Order of the British Empire for his outstanding leadership and service in WWII.

Growing up, Johnny developed a love for sports and attended many baseball games and Sunday doubleheaders either on his own or with Uncle Harold. Blue Laws mandated that games couldn't begin until after 2 PM on Sundays, so he would go to 6:30 AM Mass, catch the 10 AM ferry, and then the five-cent subway would drop him off at either the Polo Grounds to see his idol Mel Ott, or Yankee Stadium. In one game, he saw Mel Ott hit a long ball for an out, and the next time up hit a 260-foot pop up for a home run because of the strange dimensions of the Polo Grounds.

Johnny saw many notable games. When he was young, he saw Babe Ruth hit a home run. He also saw the great pitcher, Dizzy Dean, pitch for the Chicago Cubs in game two of the 1938 World Series against the Yankees. It became known as "Ol' Diz's Last Stand." He saw Brooklyn Dodger Al Gionfriddo's famous catch robbing Joe DiMaggio of a key extra base hit in the 6th game of the 1947 World Series. The normally calm DiMaggio shook his head and kicked at the dirt in frustration. Johnny was blocked by a pole at Yankee Stadium and missed the catch, but saw DiMaggio's uncharacteristic and famous reaction.

His favorite sporting events to attend were Army-Navy football games. But the most famous football game he went to was on Sunday, December 7, 1941. It was his sixteenth birthday, and he celebrated by attending the New York-Brooklyn Dodgers NFL football game at the Polo Grounds (at the time, both the MLB and NFL teams from Brooklyn were called the Dodgers). It was Tuffy Leeman Day in honor of the star for the New York Giants in the 1930s, who would later be inducted into the NFL Hall of Fame player. The game program, which Johnny held on to throughout the rest of his life, cost only ten cents. He paid for game tickets and programs with his job as the best babysitter in town, as he called himself, making fifty cents an hour.

William Donovan, the head of the Office of Strategic Services, precursor of the CIA, was in attendance, and repeated calls went out to him over the loudspeaker during the second quarter. Gradually, a buzz went through the crowd as the word slowly spread about the attack on Pearl Harbor. In the 4th quarter, an announcement was made that all service members needed to report to their commanding officer the next morning. By then, everyone knew we were at war.

In 1943, Johnny graduated from Curtis High School in New York City, where he was the manager of the high school football team since he was too small to play on the team. His main job was to make sure the shower water was hot for the players after practice. Failure to do so meant being thrown in the cold shower, but that never happened because Johnny made sure the water was always hot. He also was the sports editor for the school paper and covered the team. His alias was Seymour Wax and his slogan was "See more with Seymour."

After high school, Johnny lived in "bachelor quarters" with Pops and Uncle Harold in New York. His father, Ruth, Mike, and Patsy lived in Virginia while he worked at the Pentagon. Johnny's loving paternal grandmother, Cecilia Ulrich Hayes, died of ovarian cancer on May 30, 1942 at age sixty. Uncle Harold was the breadwinner for his parents since Pops had only owned a storage garage and tavern, and Johnny did most of the cooking for the three men in the house. While living there, Johnny started attending Stevens Institute of Technology in Hoboken to become a mechanical engineer. Johnny had hoped to go to the Naval Academy but poor eyesight disqualified him, so he took a leave from Stevens in 1944 and joined the Army.

He started his military career out in infantry school. The only time Johnny ever shot a gun was in training, and he shot everything from flamethrowers to machine guns to automatic rifles. On the range, he shot carbons at 200 yards and was judged a sharpshooter. However, he never needed to use a gun and never owned one.

Soon he went to Edgewood, thirty miles outside of Baltimore, where he worked on smoke generators. The smoke was harmless but it blanketed a drive-in movie theatre ten miles away. He later worked on dropping chemical weapons into foxholes and caves. The goal was to kill the Japanese soldiers and a month later send decomposition units in to clean up. The main motivation for developing the chemical weapons in Europe was to deter Hitler from using his, but the US leaders thought it too inhumane. But of course then they dropped the atomic bombs, so go figure.

They trained on an obstacle course and for some odd reason they used real mustard gas. They wore gas masks but when a soldier began to sweat, it would get loose and they would inhale some of the gas. Johnny would have a sore throat for days after each training. One time, the gas ended up getting in his drinking water, and he subsequently wet his pants when he went out that night. Fortunately for him, it was raining hard and no one noticed because his pants got completely wet from the rain.

Johnny was then sent to the University of Kentucky for six months to study water supplies. He went to Mass every Sunday as he always did, and played a lot of basketball with his buddies in the main gym where the great Kentucky teams played. He and a big Jewish friend got an A during the first marking period because most of it was review. Then they got a B in the second marking period, and in the third marking period, they really struggled. The teacher said he was concerned and didn't know what to do help Johnny and his friend because their grades had gotten worse. "The best I could do for you is give you a B," he said. They were thrilled - to fail meant they would be given a rifle and sent back to the infantry to fight the Nazis in Germany.

Later, they were given the option of joining a new program but they weren't told what it was. But they were again told they would be sent back to the infantry and on to Germany if they failed the program. Johnny said no to joining the program and was sent to Mississippi instead to work on water treatments for ships. He found out later that the other program was the Manhattan Project, the top secret program to develop an atomic weapon.

He was in the Army from 1944-46. When his Army duty ended, he, Pops, and Uncle Harold moved in with Johnny's dad on Long Island in Rockville Centre, known as a place where "the average mortal can live happily." This was the first time he really got to know his half-siblings Patsy and Mike. His father retired from the Navy in 1946 with regrets over not rising above Captain to Admiral. He then went to work at Todd Shipyards as a general manager. It was at this time that he and twenty-year-old Johnny finally reunited, with the exception of one brief summer in Philadelphia many years before that. They shared that Rockville Centre house with his dad's new family and adorable dog Iggy.

Thanks to the newly created G.I. Bill, Johnny re-enrolled at Stevens Institute, which he graduated from in 1948. To get to Stevens, he took the train or subway from his home on Staten Island to catch the thirty-minute ferry to New York. When it arrived in New York, people lined up to get off and then ran to the subway. Others would get on the bus. He would take another ferry to Hoboken, and then finish the journey by walking six blocks to Stevens. He and Kevin O'Neill, his best friend and future best man in his wedding, figured out how to just walk on and not to pay for the ferry rides. In all the time they spent at Stevens, they only got caught once or twice. Perhaps because Johnny and Kevin had slides rules (mechanical analog computers) with them the workers knew they were college students and allowed them to ride for free.

Some of Johnny's fondest memories were from his time as a college student living in New York. Kevin was from the Bronx, and he and Johnny would sometimes meet at Maxwell Coffee Donut House in the City and walk around Times Square. While at Stevens, Johnny sold the NY Times to students and covered the lacrosse games for the school newspaper. He later said if he had to do life over again, he might have pursued sports writing.

Johnny's younger half-sister Patsy adored her big brother, although she wasn't sure the feeling was mutual because she tended to somehow always intervene with him and his friends. His close college friend, Warren Ravioli, or "Ravi," would drag Patsy feet first up the stairs – because she asked him to! Another time, after being out all night and turning in at 2 AM, Johnny and a friend decided to sleep at his dad's house. At 7 AM, Patsy ran into the room and jumped on the friend, who she had never met before. He was startled awake suffering from the same hangover Johnny had!

He was a good brother to Mike, who looked up to Johnny as well. Johnny introduced Mike to sports and Mike became an avid sports fan from then on. Johnny took Mike to hockey, football, basketball, and baseball game, and they bonded together over frequent games of catch.

In his spare time, Johnny, like the rest of us, listened to radio shows like Fibber McGee, Milton Barley, and *The Toast of the Town* (which later became the popular Ed Sullivan television show). He enjoyed the Paul White Orchestra and songs like "Rhapsody in Blue."

He met Patty right after he graduated from Stevens, while he was in a two-year training program at Todd Shipyards in the Combustion Division. Patty worked at Todd in the accounting office as a key punch operator, which was the precursor of today's computers. She lived at home in Hoboken and was active in the Children of Mary Society and the CYO dramatics group. He was twenty-four and she was nineteen. Interestingly, there was a Todd Shipyards location in Brooklyn, which was much closer to his home, and it would have been easier for him to work there than at the Hoboken Todd Shipyards. But as fate would have it in their love story, he said he was meant to work in the Hoboken location because he met Patty there, who he called "the pretty girl at Todd."

His first date with Patty was a basketball game at Madison Square Garden on March 25, 1950 to watch national power New York City College play Bradley. However, that date almost didn't happen. She was so excited all day long for the date. He asked her out on a Friday two weeks earlier. Patty thought that the date was the prior Saturday, March 18th. Mildred and I watched her get ready as she applied her red lipstick and slipped on her favorite pearl necklace. As the proper sisters we were, we teased her that he probably wouldn't show up since he was a New York City boy. Well, in fact he did not show up, and Patty was devastated! Mildred and I felt terrible for teasing her. She later found out that he meant the next Saturday and said that she had gotten confused. Knowing both Johnny and Patty though, I'm quite sure he explained it wrong. She forgave him though, and they had a first date for the books. His first thought about her that night was, "Wow, what a sweet girl!"

Their second date was at the Bayonne Roller Rink. He picked her up in his family's 1948 black Plymouth, and while they were at the roller rink, the car's hubcaps were stolen. That same car later survived firecrackers exploding underneath it during wild Sunday Italian celebrations in Hoboken.

Patty and Johnny loved to go to $5 Broadway shows. When they were married, they would go to dinner, see a Broadway play, and pay a babysitter for under $25. They also enjoyed seeing the very funny and talented comedic piano player Victor Borge, and also went to Yankees baseball games.

Johnny would torment me by constantly teasing me and playing tricks on me! He would pat me on the back and say, "Guess who's back?" I would say, "Mine." He would say, "No, me." He would ask me again and I would say, "You," and he would say, "No, yours." I couldn't win! He would say, "Mississippi - spell it." I would spell Mississippi and he would say, "No. IT." He would do something like this every time he saw me. But I loved him!

The first time Johnny rode with Patty on the subway he wanted to protect her, so he stood right behind her as they waited in line so he could keep an eye on her and help her through the crowd onto the subway. The doors opened and the next thing he knew, she was pushing, elbowing, and shoving her way through, getting on the subway well before he did. He realized then that in addition to her being kind and considerate of everyone, she was also tough and independent.

Johnny and Patty were engaged after just three months of dating. There was no intention or plan for how he asked her. "It just popped out of my mouth," he remembered. Mildred and Jim had waited three years to be engaged, while Doris and Frank had dated just three weeks when they got engaged. Johnny was commenting to Patty one day that he thought that three months of dating was not long enough to be engaged, but Patty said it was - so right then and there, he popped the question! He jokingly said, "I had no choice. I trapped myself." They had an enjoyable engagement party at our house and we gave her a lovely bridal shower as well.

Sometime after that, she started working at Prudential in New York City. Patty was trying to save for some personal things she wanted after she became engaged, but Mother always demanded her paycheck every week. I know Patty felt very embarrassed to not have some type of trousseau to bring into her marriage.

Back then, Catholics weren't allowed to get married during Lent. The excited couple didn't want to wait until after Easter to get married, so they got married in January. It was a pleasant, crisp day, the perfect weather for a beautiful wedding. As the eldest sister, Mildred served as Patty's maid of honor. Patty was radiant, overjoyed, and stunning in her gorgeous wedding gown that Mother handmade. When the newlyweds opened their gifts, they were surprised to open two waffle irons. At the time, they wondered what to do with two, but as it turned out with their future large family, two waffle irons were perfect!

Sadly, they learned that January weddings don't always lead to the best honeymoons in New England, as theirs was almost a fatal disaster. While driving on an icy mountain road in Vermont, their car slid and almost fell off the edge of a cliff before Johnny gained control and averted a tragedy. God truly protected them.

Johnny traveled often with his work, so Patty and I would arrange to meet at Penn Station to take the train out to Queens. The first five months they were married, he worked in Philadelphia all week. He would get home Saturday night and leave Monday morning, so I would stay with Patty from Friday night until Monday and take the train back into New York. I don't know what Mother did without us in the house, but I took any and all opportunities to be away. Eventually, Patty and Johnny bought a house in Stewart Manor on Long Island and we continued to spend lots of time together, even after the babies started coming.

When their firstborn, Katherine, was born nine months and three days after their wedding date, Johnny's friend gave him a hard time. "What took you so long?" he asked. But, Katherine was also born three weeks prematurely. When Patty was pregnant with Katherine, she took a walk around West Point, which she liked to do with good weather because the fall colors were so nice. The following Monday, her water broke.

Johnny's dad adored Patty and considered his son very lucky to have her. Patsy, who was twelve at the time her idolized big brother got married, says Patty was "a saint from the very beginning." Of course, many people have said that about Patty during the course of her life. She is the most considerate person you could ever meet. If she calls someone on the phone, she starts with "Did I get you at the wrong time?" She hardly ever says a bad thing about anyone, and does everything with a strong heart and positivity.

She would go on to be a great wife, mother, and grandmother, too. She put her husband and children first. She eventually had ten children and treated each specially and uniquely. She was always worrying about her family, but never complained. Mildred and I were jealous of her youthful looks and the fact that she looked like she never aged. When she was twenty-nine and the mother of six children, she and Johnny were out to a rare night out together when she was asked for her ID when she ordered a glass of wine!

For their first Thanksgiving together, the turkey came apart in the oven. It was just Patty, John, and Uncle Harold, and she handled it like she handles everything else – calmly and well-mannered. When her second-born, Brian, was born, they moved into a detached house in Stewart Manor. It was two stories, had a dining room and kitchen, and maybe three or four bedrooms. For Patty, that was a huge step up from the apartment we grew up in in Hoboken! They had five children in six years. It would take Johnny and Patty fifteen minutes to bundle them up to go outside and play in the cold. But after two minutes, the kids wanted back in the house.

At Todd, Johnny often went out on sea trials. Occasionally, he went out of Bathe Iron Works in Maine where they were still making destroyers as they had in WWII. The Leader was built there. He was on the sea trial of the USS McCain in 1951, named after the father of the future Arizona senator and presidential candidate, John McCain.

While in New York, Johnny's boss Perry Haines needed him to go to work in Houston because Perry's wife got cancer. Perry needed Johnny there so Perry could stay in New York with his sick wife. At first, Johnny commuted occasionally from New York to Houston and still continued to work in New York and New Jersey. But eventually, he went to Houston full-time, so Patty and Johnny had to move away from their family on the east coast. Patty said a difficult and emotional goodbye, especially to Daddy, and they packed up and moved their five kids to Houston. Johnny's dad, who in 1946 became a general sales manager of Todd Shipyards in New York City, said, "I need you to go to Washington [state]." So right away, he was gone the first two weeks after they moved to Houston.

Poor Patty. She was a city girl who was now a country girl since Houston wasn't that developed yet. She was only twenty-six, looked like a teenager still, didn't drive at that time, had five children under the age of six to care for, was in a new situation that she knew little about, and was all alone for the first two weeks. After that, Johnny would typically leave on a Sunday night and work through Tuesday or Thursday. But too many times, he called to say he would have to stay another week or two. That call was always difficult and emotional for Patty. It was all really hard on her. She stuck through it though, and found a good neighbor in Joyce Banks. Joyce was a saving grace for her and helped her get through those first two weeks, as well as later on. Patty ended up loving Houston.

Sundays were a day to take the family of six young kids to a steakhouse, where for fifty cents or even free, each kid would have steak, a baked potato, garlic bread, and a drink. Years later when the family expanded to ten kids, all-you-can-eat buffets would cringe when they saw the Hayes family walk through the door.

Patty and John moved again four years later when he was promoted to District Manager of Todd's West Coast office in San Pedro Channel near Los Angeles. This move could have been to Chicago, New England, or San Francisco. Just as with the move to Houston, they didn't discuss it much. They understood that they went where Todd sent them, and Patty was again supportive because it was what was best for the family. They had bowled together in leagues in Houston and continued to so in every new city, hauling the kids around in two station wagons.

They first lived in a new community in Garden Grove and enjoyed living there. Four years later, they moved to Bakersfield when Johnny left Todd to start his own business. When that failed after one year, he began working for future NBA Hall of Famer George Yardley in Long Beach two hours away. Since 1960 the George Yardley company has been at the forefront of providing engineered energy and efficiency solutions for buildings throughout the southwest United States.

When they weren't able to sell the house in Bakersfield, they decided to let Katherine finish her education at Foothill High School. Johnny commuted for three years, coming home only on weekends. Patty again did a heroic job raising a family that had doubled to ten children, (including eight boys) and their favorite dog Sydney, while tolerating Bakersfield (what some call "the armpit of California").

Johnny thrived at the Yardley Company and held his boss and his family in the highest esteem. He had memorable contracts doing work at Epcot, Petco Park, the Honda Center, Los Angeles Convention Center, and the dolphin pool at SeaWorld in San Diego. The family had grown to ten with the birth of Matthew in Bakersfield. When asked why they had so many kids, Johnny answered, "The rich get richer and the poor have kids. We have a Johnny, a Matthew, and we're trying for a Mark and a Luke. We started trying for a basketball team, and then once we had a basketball team, we thought about having a football team." Patty referred to Johnny as her eleventh child, so I guess they had a football team after all!

Johnny enjoyed telling this funny story:

"Mrs. O'Donovan was walking down O'Connell Street in Dublin, and coming in the opposite direction was Father Rafferty. 'Hello,' said the Father, 'and how is Mr. O'Donovan? Didn't I marry you two years ago?'

She replied, 'That you did, Father.'

The priest asked, 'And are there any little ones yet?'

'No, not yet Father,' said she.

'Well, now, I'm going to Rome next week, and I'll light a candle for you.'

A few years later they met again. 'Well, now, Mrs. O'Donovan,' said the Father, 'How are you?'

'Oh, very well,' said she.

'And tell me,' he said, 'Have you any little ones yet?'

'Oh yes, Father. I've had three sets of twins, and four singles – ten in all.'

'Now isn't that wonderful,' he said, 'And how is your lovely husband?'

'Oh,' she said, 'He's gone to Rome – to blow out the damn candles!'"

The Hayes clan moved every four years over a twelve-year period of time. Johnny and Patty used to joke that every time the local Catholic Church built a new church and a new freeway was built, they knew it was time to move. But on July 1, 1969, they made their final move. They bought a brand-new house across from an orange grove in Placentia, California. They would add a big family room to that house. It became a favored and loved home to grandchildren, great-grandchildren, and their kids' friends for many years. Many in the family have memories of the smell of coffee in the morning and coming downstairs to see Johnny ("Poppa") reading the morning paper and Patty ("Grandma") doing her crossword puzzles at the kitchen table.

Patty had to be both a loving mother and a disciplinarian, especially with eight boys. Johnny said she was responsible for 80% or more of the raising of the children, and she was the best mother there was. One cherished tradition was when Johnny would play quarterback in family touch football games in the street or backyard, and afterwards, Patty would clean up the cuts and scrapes that came from those games. Although he loves his children, his love for Patty is greater and comes first above everything else.

She truly is an amazing mother and it is her passion and life's calling. Her life is centered on her family and it is a full-time job that she has done for a lifetime, 24/7, without any time off and with no work holidays. She was a mother to ten teenagers and lived to tell! She has become a role model for younger women, including George Yardley's daughter-in-law, Linda. She inspires her children to be loving parents as well. She is a gifted mother who affirms and loves each of her ten children as if each is an only child and with unconditional love. She knows what each needs and when, has a sixth sense of how each is doing, rejoices in their successes and accomplishments and who they grew to become, hurts and worries when they struggle or are hurting, and prays devotedly and even anxiously at times for each child.

In addition to caring for her children, she honored and loved our parents and Johnny's family. She cared for Uncle Harold in his later years and for her father-in-law, even when he struggled with alcohol. She loves her children's spouses as her own children, and eventually, her fifteen grandchildren. Through the years she washed countless clothes, cooked countless huge meals, and drove countless miles taking kids everywhere, doing it all with love and joy.

The Hayes home is open to all as is her refrigerator! A few of her children's friends used to walk in unannounced and head straight to the kitchen. All are welcome - family, friends, groups, and strangers. Her open and loving heart warms the house. She hugs people as they enter and exit the house, and waves from the lawn as they drive off. Her house is a refuge and a place of love, rest, and peace for her adult children to get away, crash on the couch, and relax and recharge.

Patty is happiest surrounded by family, especially grandchildren. She loves it when they all are enjoying a meal at the house or a favorite restaurant, and she cherishes time when the family is at church together. The Hayes house is full on special occasions - Easter, Thanksgiving, and especially Christmas Eve and Day which she plans all year for (Christmas is important to her because Daddy made it special for us growing up). Patty has beautiful olive skin and is vibrant with joy and love, but her happiness shows the most when she is surrounded by her family. She considers herself to be truly blessed by her children, their spouses, and her grandchildren.

Patty has a pure and genuine faith through all life's circumstances, and it is her ultimate source of strength and hope. It overflows out of a love for Christ which began early in her life and remains a consistent foundation. She sees Christ in every person and worth in all as God's children. She shows the love of Christ as St. Francis explains: "Tell all of the love of Christ and use words if necessary." It hurts her when she is criticized for "just being a mom" but in the midst of the feminist movement, she still follows Jesus' mother Mary as her feminine example. She still walks to church every morning where she continues to draw strength and inspiration from the truths we learned growing up in Hoboken.

Now that the kids are grown and have left the house, Johnny and Patty go to dinner and a movie every weekend unless grandchildren come to visit. They make trips to Laughlin where Patty plays the penny slots, always wins, and always knows when to stop. They are thriving in that community. Johnny and Patty were elected to the El Dorado High School Athletic Hall of Fame in 2000 for their service to the school alongside Olympic swimming great Janet Evans and major league baseball star Phil Nevin. Pat was also a finalist for Placentia Woman of the Year for her service to her church and community. She is loved and appreciated by all.

Mick and Me

After graduating from high school in 1950, I got a job working in the financial district of New York. I had only just turned seventeen and I worked for a diamond broker. Our office was directly on the Hudson River and my view from my desk was of the Statue of Liberty. That New York City office building that I worked in was later torn down, along with many others, in order to build the Twin Towers complex.

I had decided that I needed to get away from home in order to make some sort of life for myself. I was working and making pretty good money at that time and I turned it all over to Mother and received only $2.50 per week for myself. Out of that I had to pay for my transportation, which was thirty cents per day. I also had to supply my lunches from this money and if I needed any stockings or any other type of clothing I had to chip in on that also, even for a new coat I desperately needed. Needless to say I walked a lot and took lunches to work to save a few cents.

I had barely turned seventeen when I was hired and I had a very stressful job. Mother had gotten me an interview with this firm in New York and I was hired the same day. I never got a chance to celebrate my graduation or take a day off. I worked for this business for two and a half years and became senior clerk.

I was all of seventeen and very unhappy. I never had time to work at home or even have a boyfriend. It was always time at work, then time to work at home, with no let up and no money to do anything with.

Finally, I decided to get a job somewhere else and leave home or move in with friends. I was so intent on this that it was becoming obsessive. One day while I was on the subway, I encountered a girl I had been good friends with but hadn't seen in years. She was in a Navy uniform and we sat together and chatted about her career. She convinced me that I should look up the recruiting office in New York City and get some information, which is exactly what I did. So I decided to quit and joined the Navy in the midst of the Korean War. Of course, that was where I met Mick and the rest is history. I never regretted that decision and would have stayed on if the Navy hadn't decided that a married woman who allowed herself to get pregnant wasn't permitted to wear the Navy uniform.

I joined the WAVES, which stands for Women Accepted for Volunteer Emergency Service, a unit of the US Naval Reserve. The WAVES' mission was to replace the men in on-shore stations so they could be sent for sea duty. Some of the men resented the WAVES because they didn't want to give up their stations.

Eleanor Roosevelt helped persuade the Navy to begin this program. Congress was slow to enact it but FDR signed it into law on July 30, 1942. They wanted women between twenty-five and thirty years old with 20/20 vision, normal auditory acuity, good speaking ability, and quick reactions in stressful situations. We were not eligible for combat duty and in 1945 there were 86,000 WAVES.

We trained for twelve intensive weeks, including eight hours a day in the classroom. There were jobs in aviation, medicine, science, technology, and communication. WAVES patched bullet holes in naval boats and performed engine checks on seaplanes. WAVES were yeomen, radio operators, storekeepers, cooks, and bakers.

The Navy provided cryptology classes at several colleges for some WAVES. Many students received their code training in a three-month course at Smith College in Massachusetts. Those whose test scores were high were sent straight to work in Washington, D.C. Women accepted into the cryptologic field were sworn to secrecy, and the penalty for discussing their work outside proper channels — considered an act of treason in time of war — could be death. It was especially important work during WWII in reading German intercepted codes.

We had to have short hair, but feminine hair-dos, and wear skirts and gloves. The Navy asked noted fashion designer Main Rousseau Bocher to create a stylish uniform. He then donated his designs to the Navy for the WAVES. Each enlistee was given four uniforms: summer greys, summer dress whites, working blues, and of course, dress blues. The uniform regulations were specific, and frequent surprise inspections were standard procedure.

At first, WAVES were often assigned to less desirable night and weekend shifts. With women working around the clock it had adverse effects on health. WAVES' sleeping quarters were comprised of several barracks that housed more than 4,000 WAVES. Eighty-four women shared one large room, sleeping in bunk beds and storing their belongings in nearby steel lockers. It became apparent to the Navy that better living conditions would foster higher morale and improve health conditions. The living quarters were then enlarged to create more privacy and better health. By the time I joined we had these better conditions, and I had a lot of fun in those dorms with fellow WAVES.

In 1951, Mick enlisted in the Marine Corps at age eighteen. He wanted to enlist earlier, but his father would not sign off on the papers. He never should have been allowed in the Marines though. The first time he tried to enlist they turned him down because his vision wasn't good enough, and for good reason. He is blind in his left eye and has been since childhood. He decided to go to a different recruiter and this time he passed with flying colors – because he memorized the entire eye chart! That's Mick for you.

Once he did enlist he was assigned to the VMF-235 Fighter Squadron in El Toro, California. He and two friends, Juan Quijano and Gregorio Gonzales Gutierrez, requested to go to Korea to fight. Mr. Quijano and Mr. Gutierrez were granted their request, but Mick received orders to attend aviation maintenance school in Jacksonville, Florida.

When I met Mick, I was in Jacksonville attending the Navy Electronics School. After classes, many of the students went to a sandwich shop to eat and that's where Mick first saw me. He saw me across the room, standing in line. He said to his friends, "I'm going to marry that girl." They all laughed and gave him a hard time. After asking around and finding out who I was, he decided to visit me in the barracks. The person at the desk called me to tell me I had a visitor on deck. But that took too long for Mick so he left (he is still so impatient!).

Mick was a red-haired Buck Sergeant and a very interesting Marine! Mick laughs whenever he tells the story because when he saw me the next day I was furious. And that same scenario played out many times. He would try to see me, it would take too long, and so he would just leave.

He is probably the only Marine to have no pants on in the WAVES barracks! One day when he came to see me he was caught in the rain and took his pants off to have them ironed. He was panicked that he was going to be caught and they wouldn't believe his story!

After school, we continued to see each other. Instead of being sent to Korea, Mick was transferred to a reserve outfit in Millington, Tennessee. As God would have it, I received orders to attend another school at the Millington Naval Air Station. Mick truly believes it was God who made it happen that he was sent to school and that we were stationed at the same place. When I graduated, Mother, Daddy, Aunt Marie, and my brother Frank all attended my graduation.

When the talks of the Korean War weren't going as well as planned, we decided to get married. If the war continued on much longer Mick would be transferred back to his unit in El Toro, California, and then on to Korea. The war would separate us and create much uncertainty.

Around this time, I found out that Mick's name wasn't really Mick Murphy! He thought that if something were to go wrong between us, I wouldn't be able to find him because he didn't give me his actual name. His friends called him "Murph," so he was able to pull it off. "Mick" is a derogatory name for Irish people so it was hilarious to his friends. When we first talked about marriage, he finally told me that his real name was Joseph … Joe. It didn't matter. His family calls him Joe but that sounds really strange to me. For me his name will always be Mick.

We were married on March 28, 1953, when we were both still nineteen, a few days from turning twenty. On the night of the wedding, our friends had a shivaree for us. A shivaree is a noisy, clamorous serenade for a newlywed couple. Included in this group were the friends who had laughed at Mick when he announced he was "going to marry this girl." They were outside our hotel room singing and banging on the windows and doors. I told Mick not to answer the door but in typical Mick fashion he said, "The hell with that" and answered the door. One of the friends, a former wrestler aptly named Popeye, burst through the door. Mick tried to hold the door but Popeye was a brute and the rowdy crowd followed him in. It was actually a lot of fun and so very memorable.

Of course, with Mick in the military, we constantly moved. We have lived in Millington, Tennessee; Gary, Indiana; Ft. Leavenworth, Kansas; Santa Ana, California; Panama Canal Zone; Bakersfield, California; Ft. Rucker, Alabama; Schofield Barracks, Hawaii; White Sands, Missile Range, New Mexico; Las Cruces, New Mexico; League City, Texas; and Surprise, Arizona.

The first places we lived in were all dumps! The very first place had an outhouse pretty far removed from the house. Mick's father, brother, sister-in-law, and sister all came over to visit and after seeing the place, they refused to stay there. The next place was right below a water tower. A big whistle blew every day at noon and sounded like a train. It was one big room with one bed in it and plenty of spiders. From there we moved to an old funeral home. The elderly man there who owned it was wonderful to us. While there, we had a puppy named Fart Blossom. Blossom became part of the family because one night Mick gambled and lost his entire paycheck. He brought the puppy home so I wouldn't be mad at him. I was still mad at him but the puppy was adorable and became a loved pet.

The Korean War ended with the signing of the truce in July of 1953. We remained in Tennessee where our first three children, Terrence, Maureen, and Michael were born. We later moved to Gary, Indiana, where Eugene and Colleen were born. Maureen died shortly after birth. She was born prematurely and the hospital made an error in her care. The results of an in-depth investigation were kept from Mick and me. The Commander of the Marine Corps told us he was truly sorry. Off the record, he said that someone had "yinged when he should have yanged." It was heartbreaking and is difficult to write about, so I will leave it at that.

During that time, Mick spent five months separated

from us while serving in Japan. One day in Japan, he and two other guys were underneath the belly of an aircraft. At the same time, another aircraft was taxiing in when its tire blew. The tire flew under the belly where they were working and killed one of the guys next to Mick. We felt terrible for his partner, but we were grateful because it could have been Mick. He was sent home after that accident.

After Colleen was born in 1959, I needed surgery for bad varicose veins that were causing poor blood circulation. My legs were wrapped in ace bandages for a while and I was in a hospital in Great Lakes. Mick requested a thirty-day medical leave to come home and take care of me and the kids. His request was granted but when he needed to extend that time, he received a telegram from the Commandant of the Marine Corps stating that if "SGT Murphy needed a hardship discharge then he needed to request one. If not then he is to report to his unit in California for deployment in three days."

Mick felt he had no choice but to leave the Marine Corps. He was disappointed because he absolutely loved the Marine Corps and was up for a promotion to Gunnery Sergeant, but our family and I needed him at home. I'm thankful he loved us so much to make that sacrifice, to leave the Marine Corps that he was so devoted to.

It turned out to be a good decision for many reasons, including news we would soon receive about little Colleen.

Mick received an Honorable Discharge on December 4, 1959, and soon began working for the City of Hammond, Indiana in the water works department. He continued for a little over a year until he refused to join the union and was terminated. By then, Colleen had been diagnosed with a serious heart problem. Mick, concerned about her having good medical care, reached out to the Marine Corps to re-enlist. He was told that, although he would keep his years of service, he would have to start over in rank.

Anyone who knows Mick would understand and maybe smile at his reaction. He told them where to go and instead

121

enlisted in the Army. Again, he made the tough decision to do what was best for the family. He was sworn in in April of 1961 and stationed at Ft. Leonard Wood, Missouri, in the Missouri Ozarks. They didn't make him go to Boot Camp or complete any training. When he was issued his uniform, he didn't know what went where. They promised him that he wouldn't be sent overseas, but after settling in he was sent to Germany. Eugene was an infant, Colleen was two, Michael four, and Terry seven.

He was in Germany for seven or eight months when someone came in the hanger yelling for "Murph." They told him to get his things together, that he was going home. I had reached out to the Red Cross for help because Colleen had to be hospitalized. Since I had to be with Colleen in the hospital, Michael and Terry were actually put in an orphanage during the hospitalization. The Army woman representative assigned to me appealed to the Army, who finally brought Mick home. Again, it was a huge help and relief to have Mick home to help.

Mick eventually served two tours in Vietnam, from 1963-64 and again in 1967-68. He was a platoon leader and a helicopter door machine gunner. Door gunners had a very difficult, dangerous, and critical job. He flew on UH-1 Iroquois choppers (Hueys) on numerous vital missions. The Huey could skim the ground over target areas like no other aircraft. Gunners mainly fired M 16s and were indispensable to chopper and crew safety.

The tight-knit crew flew a variety of critical missions during the day but also at night because the Viet Cong liked to move and attack at night. The air express choppers were "Johnny on the run," delivering critical water supplies, rations, fuel, radio parts …you name it. They would also transport Vietnamese women and children (who may or may not have been friendly) from their homes to safety out of Viet Cong-controlled villages.

They also provided vital air coverage for convoys in Viet Cong strongholds. But they were most vulnerable when they had to deliver and pick up troops. The bigger Chinook 47 choppers specialized in these types of missions. It is still painful for Mick to think about because he remembers so many young faces and he knew when they were dropping them off that a lot of them weren't going to come back alive.

The most rewarding missions were those to pick up and transport wounded American and Vietnamese soldiers to field hospitals. However, these were also very hairy situations because it was typical of the Viet Cong to attack during these medevac operations. They were like sitting ducks so they couldn't waste any time getting in, loading the patients, and getting out. It was hard to see the pain, agony, and even death of soldiers. Still, transporting the wounded was the most rewarding part of the job, especially when lives were saved.

Oftentimes, I would watch the war coverage on the news and I knew in my heart, at that moment, Mick was flying in the face of danger, especially when they were around the DMZ. I prayed, and worried, and prayed some more. I tried to stay strong and hopeful until I could talk to him and hear his voice. But it was still very hard at times.

As platoon sergeant, Mick was in command over a group of men. One time he went into the barracks in Vietnam and they were smoking pot. He told them that he would not tolerate anything like that... walked away and never saw it again. That is so like Mick.

As platoon sergeant, he was issued a 45 and just for the fun of it, he also had a plastic 45 that looked just like the real one. They regularly had equipment inspections and as always when one came up, he ran and retrieved his 45. But one time he ran back to the inspection only to find out that he had grabbed the plastic gun instead. He laughs as he recounts seeing the look on the warrant officer and inspector's faces when they inspected his firearm and realized it was plastic. He was really chewed out for that one because he was the senior man for his platoon.

Later, he was injured during a run when fuel leaked from

the tailstock and burned his hand. They were in the middle of a mission, flying between Nha Trang, Saigon, Da Nang, and the Mekong Delta. The fuel burnt his hand and they continued the mission but by the afternoon, his hand was seriously swollen. They flew him to a medical site where they did surgery and sent him home to heal.

I didn't tell the kids he was coming home so that it was a special surprise for them. Colleen's class was out on the playground. Her teacher smiled, gave her keys to Colleen, and told her to get her things out of the classroom and then go to the office. As Colleen ran out of the classroom onto the dry dirt in the direction of the office, she saw her older brother Michael. He was running toward the office from the opposite direction. They laughed at each other and began to race and when they met in the center and turned the corner, they saw Mick. Michael was ecstatic and reached Mick first and they embraced. Colleen was absolutely sobbing and couldn't stop. Mick kept asking her why she was crying. That is so Mick as well!

It was a wonderful reunion. Patty's family was able to see him as well and spend time with him. His hand was fully bandaged but he looked great otherwise. Patty's son Greg got to thank him for sending a jar of Vietnam sand that Mick had sent him to show his third grade class.

Mick returned to Vietnam after a couple of weeks. On a later run the chopper went up but they couldn't get enough height for whatever reason and it came down hard on its right side. It was a big helicopter, which meant it was a big drop. Mick was the gunner on the left and was responsible for seeing that everyone made it out of the chopper. He had to be the last one out. The gunner on the right side, who was a big guy, was pinned under the door. Mick and the others scrambled to get out and free the right gunner. He was finally able to crawl out from under the chopper. They then vacated the area as fast as they could because they believed the chopper was going to explode.

Mick says the only thing hurt was his pride. Afterwards,

he sat on the ground and cried like a baby. As the chopper was crashing, he saw all of his kids and me by myself. He "knew his time was up" and was "scared s---less." Another chopper picked them up, brought them back to base, and then they jumped on another one and continued on to dangerous missions. Such is life in war.

Mick insists he did nothing heroic and that he was just doing his job, but the Army brass knew it was heroic. They awarded him the Bronze Star for his brave actions. Mick's Airman's Medal, the Marine Corps Medal, and the Bronze Medal are hanging in a shadow box in our home in Arizona. The kids grew up seeing those medals but were too young to really understand that Mick served with such honor and distinction.

All soldiers serving in combat were eligible for a seven-day pass to Hawaii. During his second tour in Vietnam, I met him in Hawaii and we had a great week together. Jimmy Murphy came and stayed with the kids who, even though they didn't see Mick, were happy that I could spend time with him.

The kids were able to talk to Mick occasionally during his time in Vietnam. The operators were so amazing with the kids. The operator would tell them when to begin, and we would have to end each side of our conversation with "over." It could get confusing for the kids since there was quite a delay. "Hi Colleen. Over." "Hi Dad! Over." (Delay.) "Are you being good for Mom? Over." "Yes, Over." We couldn't talk long because there were so many of us, but it was still great to hear Mick's voice.

Maybe my very favorite story about Mick involves a fight at the NCO Club. Army personnel and Marines were arguing about whose medals were better, and it broke into an all-out brawl. Chairs and fists were flying. They sent the riot squad to break it up and everyone ran.

Mick and three friends hid in the car for a while and then decided to hide in the shrubs. The Military Police (MP) saw him, walked up with a flashlight, and told him to "Come out of there, you SOB." He explained that he needed to notify me, so two MPs escorted him to our house, where he knocked on the door. When I opened the door, Mick was standing there with an MP on each elbow. He smiled and said, "Honey, I won't be home tonight."

The next morning he went before the "Old Man," as they called the Commanding Officer, who was not happy. He gave Mick grief about being the senior man present and yelled, "If you weren't married with all those kids I'd bust your ass right now!"

Mick was confined to the barracks for thirty days. But after Taps played each evening, Mick would walk out, jump the fence, and go home to us. Then, he would get up early the next morning and return before anyone knew. Early one morning, when he was walking back, the commanding officer was in a car driving by. He had the driver stop and asked Mick what he was doing. Mick told him he was "getting some exercise." The "Old Man" just gave him a look and told the driver to go on.

He was a wild one when he was young. Of course, he is nothing like that now. He is still bold and still seemingly fearless but also the epitome of integrity. He was and is still quite a colorful man. What's funny is that he had no patience for any of the things he did when it came to our children. One minute late, one week's restriction. Two minutes, two weeks. They always, always, had to be dressed, say, "yes sir, yes ma'am, no sir, no ma'am." He was a man of rules! Colleen laughs about that now.

I remember one huge fight we had. The kids were all in their rooms and Mick and I were in the living room. We had just received word that Mick was probably going to go back to Vietnam for a third tour. We had several neighbors on post who had never been to Vietnam and I wasn't having it. THEY needed to go to Nam! I asked him how he could leave his family again. His reply goes around in my head to this day. He told me, "My country comes first, then my wife and kids." That was hard for the kids to swallow and understand then, but they would understand and appreciate it later in life. He explained that without serving his country, he wouldn't be able to keep us all safe, free, fed, and healthy. I wish more people felt that way... and especially actress Jane Fonda! I will abhor her to my dying day for how she disrespected our soldiers. I love Mick so much and am fiercely devoted to him! And he sacrificed so much for me and our family, as well as our country. But we are also thankful he didn't go back for that third term.

Mick ended his time in the Army in 1973. He enrolled at New Mexico State University near our home in Las Cruces. In 1976, he graduated with a degree in Business Administration. I was so proud of him learning alongside the younger college students. He was then hired as Director of Administrative Services in League City, Texas. Mick was an excellent city administrator at that job. We lived there until he retired from that job in 1996 and then after a brief time seeing the country in an RV, we moved to our retirement community in Surprise, Arizona.

CHAPTER 6

HOBOKEN TRAGEDY

During his first term in Vietnam, I lived in Santa Ana with the kids, very close to where Patty lived in Garden Grove. That was a wonderful time for us to be together and for the cousins to get to know each other. That was also where our youngest child, Kathleen, was born.

During Mick's second tour of duty in Vietnam we moved to Bakersfield to again be near Patty and Johnny. When we first got to Bakersfield, all sixteen of our kids (all sixteen years and younger), twelve boys and four girls, lived in Johnny and Patty's house. Since Mick was in Vietnam and Johnny was staying in Long Beach two hours away for work all week, Patty and I took care of the children with the help of Patty's oldest, Katherine (named after Johnny's mom and with all her wonderful qualities). It was, of course, quite a challenge and could be hectic at times. Eventually we got our own house, but it was very special being with my best friend and sister and having our children all together in one house.

It was also very special that Mildred's oldest son Jimmy lived with Patty's family after graduating from high school. He attended Bakersfield College and became big brother to Patty's ten kids, and later our six while we lived there too. Patty loved having Jimmy there as they had always had a special and loving bond. With Jimmy there, it helped Patty feel a special Kennedy connection that she had missed since moving away.

We were together in the same house in Bakersfield on June 18, 1967, when we received the call that Daddy had passed away from prostate cancer at age seventy-six. It was such a hard and emotional phone call but it was also very good for us to be together to share the grief. Patty took it the hardest. She cried and cried over the loss of Daddy, who she absolutely truly adored and loved and with whom she shared so many admirable qualities. With Johnny and Mick both gone, we needed to be there for the sixteen kids, so we were not able to fly back for the funeral. That was hard but we had no choice and so we supported each other, and the demands of sixteen kids kept us busy and preoccupied.

Daddy was still a police officer when he got his prostate cancer diagnosis. He was legally blind and yet still worked a busy intersection of 14th and Washington. Somehow, he still managed to do his job. Whenever he was off duty and saw a police officer directing traffic, he would walk out into the street and carry on a conversation with him.

When he was diagnosed with his illness, we knew that he might not make it. He had no hobbies. He was a city guy. He loved being a police officer but when he got sick, he could not do his job any longer. He lived for that and it gave him purpose. He was proud to be a police officer and we were proud of him. One of my most prized possessions is Daddy's patrol books from all those years as a police officer, in which he wrote everything down.

He was such a good and compassionate police officer. The people in town loved him and called him "Pat." Everyone, including his three sons-in-law, would tell you he had a heart of gold. He was the old, friendly, humble Irish cop who had nothing bad to say about anyone and was kind and considerate of everyone. When he passed, some of the homeless men came to his funeral. It was a fitting tribute to him. They wore what they had, nothing fancy, and told Mother and Mildred how much he meant to them. Daddy would sit at the piers overlooking the Hudson River and just spend time with them. They had great appreciation for him.

Mother and Daddy would visit us every summer, first wherever we were and then with Patty and Johnny. Mick had little patience with Mother but Daddy was always patient with Mother. She would constantly criticize, nag, and even yell at him, but he didn't take the bait and go back at her. Mick would say she would "nip at his ankles."

Mick had a bowling team and one night Daddy went with him to watch. They were out later than expected and when they returned, Mother and I were waiting on the stairway for them. Mother just started in and was really getting into Daddy. But he just smiled and they walked to their room, where she just kept on really giving it to him. So Mick yelled into the room "Hit her Pat, hit her!" Of course, he wasn't serious. He was just stirring the pot but it is still funny to think about.

After Daddy passed away, it was just Mother who visited every summer, except for the time she brought her friend, Sister Agnes Jane, with her. Mother would often say "No one wants me here, so I'll go home." One summer Mick had had enough and actually packed her bags, kicked her out, and sent her a few weeks early to Patty and Johnny. Johnny was much more patient and tolerant with her but one time when she threatened to leave, he told her, "OK. You can leave." Patty, ever the family peacemaker, remained loving always.

But in fairness to Mother, she mellowed later in life. She played card games, Yahtzee, and dominoes with the younger grandchildren. Mildred and her family did the best they could do to care for her but she still struggled with loneliness as she lived alone in her apartment. We talked to her for years about moving into a senior center and when she finally did she loved it. But she got sick soon thereafter and passed away in 1988 at age eighty-four.

She loved God, her children, and her grandchildren. She told me, "All the grandchildren are not only good children but are well situated jobwise. I am very proud of my family." She had a bracelet with a charm for each of her twenty-five grandchildren. You could always hear her coming with her jangling bracelet. She prayed the rosary three times a day and prayed for all of her grandchildren each day. She said her goal was to "lead a good life and love God to the best of my ability." Mother did that to the very end, as she did many years earlier in the midst of a terrible tragedy.

Frank and Doris

Frank was a well-liked, popular star running back at St. Michael's. After graduation in 1943, he enlisted in the Marines at the age of seventeen and went to boot camp in North Carolina. He saw service at Bougainville Island in Papua, New Guinea, and then in China because the United States and China were allies against Japan in the China-Burma-India theatre. The Marines were ordered to participate in the occupation of parts of China to assist Chiang Kai-shek's government in the surrender and disarmament of the Japanese troops.

But the original plan was for Frank and his fellow Marines to be part of the massive amphibious assault of Japan. The bombing of Hiroshima and Nagasaki and the surrender of the Japanese changed those plans. Eventually he would get to Japan as part of the occupation force there.

After serving for three and a half years, Frank was honorably discharged from the Marines. Frank's first job was to chauffeur Freeholder Robert Emery, and then he joined the Hudson County Boulevard Police.

He met Doris Manzo and they were married after being engaged for only three weeks. At first, Frank and Doris had a big apartment but had to move out of it because it was too expensive. They moved into a smaller apartment but then bought the biggest refrigerator they could find, but it wouldn't fit because it was so big. Frank, a very talented musician, on occasion played several instruments in a corps band, the Hawthorne Cavaliers of Hawthorne. Like Daddy, Frank was a dapper dresser, and he always carried a 9mm pistol in an ankle holster.

In 1954, he left the Hoboken police force. He applied for and was appointed to the Hudson County police, but decided not to take the job. He started to work at a Modern Motors used car lot, where he had a reputation as a better-than-average salesman. Some used car lots in New Jersey were known to have a gangster affiliation.

Meanwhile, things were not going well with Doris. Sadly, Frank and Doris separated after the birth of their second son Keith, born November 27, 1955. Things became especially hard on Doris, a young wife and mother. A year or so later, she unexpectedly became pregnant with their third child.

It was lonely and humiliating for Doris to be pregnant with a child whose father seemingly had no interest in her. She was forced to go to doctors' appointments at facilities for single women, poor blacks, and other minorities. It was embarrassing to have to go to court for back payments two days before she went into labor and gave birth to Brian on October 5, 1957. Doris would later say that she was very naïve at the time. She became increasingly bitter and her anger would cause her problems for years to come.

In December of 1958, Frank was living with Mother and Daddy and running around with other women. They had been estranged for about two years and Doris was living at the Union City housing project at 861 39th St. with their three young children. Nonetheless, Doris' father, Anthony Manzo, was hoping they would reconcile. Frank was a fairly frequent visitor and had been with the boys at Christmas in 1958.

In the early morning hours of New Year's Day, 1959, Frank was driving with his then girlfriend, 22 year old divorcee Elisabeth London (apparently, she was involved with several men), and one of the co-owners of the used car lots, 42 year old Henry Knipper. They were together in a pink Cadillac after ushering in the New Year by barhopping. Frank would normally go home with her to her house but tonight she strangely told him to drop her off and drive home to his parents' house instead.

Around 2:30 AM, a black car that had tailed Frank from as far away as North Bergen forced Frank to the side of the road at an intersection, a maneuver called "curbing." A second car drew abreast of Frank as he waited for the light to shift.

A man in the passenger seat of that second car pulled out a black .38 caliber pistol and fired two shots to the closed driver-side window of the Cadillac. One hit Frank in the left shoulder, lodging there. The other bullet hit his left eye, killing him instantly.

The scene was only a few minutes' ride from our parents' home and only two blocks from the Second Precinct Station, where Daddy was assigned. John Stewart, state motor vehicle inspector on routine holiday road duty, found Frank's still-warm body slumped over in the driver's seat. All the doors in the car were locked and the windows were up. His feet were on the pedals and the motor was running with the car in gear.

His body was taken to the local morgue, where at 7:30 AM. Daddy sadly had to identify him. A priest from Our Lady of Grace Church gave him last rites.

The local newspaper would soon take a picture of his body in the car and splash it across the front page of the newspapers. It was terrible and they would continue to run a story about Frank's murder on the front page of the newspaper for the next six New Year's Day editions.

The papers described Frank as a handsome, tall, strapping, wavy-haired ex-cop who had once been a star football player, and sensationalized the murder with big, bold headlines:

"Ex-Cop Ambushed, Slain Gang-Style in His Caddy"

"NJ Cops Baffled by 'Pro' Slaying of Ex-Policeman"

"Auto Deals Linked to Gang-Style Slaying of Ex-Cop in Hoboken"

"Kennedy Slaying Stumps Police; Mistaken Identity, Dad Thinks." A smaller headline read "Castro Enters Havana: Civil War Victor Picks Urritia to Succeed Batista."

Both Hudson County and Hoboken police launched an investigation, led by Chiefs George Bouille and Edgar Scott. Scott called the shooting "a professional job." Police spent all day questioning relatives, business associates, and friends, trying to learn something that might lead them to the assassin and a motive. Modern Motors owned the car in which Frank was killed. Both Miss London and Knipper were held as material witnesses with bail set at $10,000 and $5,000 respectively. One of the many questioned and released was Carmine Falconieri, trumpet player in the Hawthorne Cavalier Band at one of the nightspots Frank had visited that night. Falconieri told police Frank had sold him his car about a year earlier.

Doris fainted when she heard the news from her father, a Hudson County fireman. He was very upset as well and spent the night with her. The rest of us each received the horrible news through frightening middle of the night phone calls. It was clearly a Mafia-style professional hit job and so in addition to the terrible news we also had to deal with that terrifying reality and uncertainty. Growing up in Hoboken, we knew all about the Mafia and that this horrific crime might never be solved. We Kennedy sisters, like Mother, can be worriers, and this gave us a real reason to be fearful.

Patty worried the most. Without knowing the exact reason for Frank's murder, Patty feared for her five young children's safety in Houston. At the time, she was pregnant with her sixth child, Patrick Joseph (named after Daddy). She carried the trauma of that middle of the night call with her forever, so much so that when one of her children called from college often her first words might be "What's the matter?" or "What's wrong?"

Frank was killed on Jim Murphy's birthday. Mildred was overcome with emotion and it was the first time her ten-year-old son Jimmy ever saw her cry. To make things even worse, people in their neighborhood made comments to Mildred that their family was Mafia. It was just so much to deal with and very unfair and cruel. It was especially overwhelming for Jimmy. He was frightened and upset seeing his mother cry for the first time and hearing neighbors say they were bad people.

Patty and I flew out for the wake. The Catholic Church would not bury him so there was no public service, which upset Mother and Mildred even more. But we maintained hope that Frank still had his faith since they found rosary beads in his pocket when he was killed.

Out of concern for her children, Mildred sent Jimmy and her younger kids to stay with Jim's parents. She didn't want them to be at the wake and see all the strong emotions. It helped them to be protected at their grandparents' house. However, his grandfather Murphy liked to watch a lot of television and news of the murder was all over TV. So even there, young Jimmy and his younger siblings were exposed to frightening news.

Frank was a big guy and even though Jimmy rarely saw him he was afraid of Frank. Jimmy remembers riding in the backseat of Frank's car. It seemed to Jimmy that Frank was driving way too fast. He would be so afraid that he would cry on the transmission hump in the backseat. Everything about this added to his fears.

Of course, the shocking murder was hardest on Doris, who understandably had the most difficult time dealing with it. She had to deal with her own emotions as well as care for and protect three young boys. Doris told her six-year-old son Kevin that his father had died in a car accident. But with all the pictures and write-ups in the local and New York papers, Kevin's little friends in their housing development told Kevin the truth. Doris was disgusted by this as she had wanted to protect Kevin, four-year-old Keith, and two-year-old Brain from the awful truth, especially since they didn't know their father well and saw him only during visiting times.

Doris took her first Social Security check of $700 and moved out of the projects. She put $650 down on a small ranch house in Bricktown, which a friend of Frank's had told her about. She used the remaining $50 to pay for a moving van and they moved there in July of 1959.

Her girlfriend Sylvia from Irvington, a divorcee with two boys, had a car, and so they all moved in together so they could pool their money and pay expenses. By chance, she met George Coupland, who was recently widowed and was on vacation and living next door with his father. George asked Doris out to dinner the day he met her and they got along really well right away. George proposed on the first, second, and third evenings they were together! Doris considered this a truly great thing for her and her three boys. They married in 1960 and two years later had a beautiful baby, Maureen.

Unfortunately, there was more heartache ahead for Doris. As much as she loved George, she gradually learned he had a serious drinking problem, which adversely affected the family and their relationship.

On March 20, 1967, George, while drunk, killed himself in a single car accident. Her difficult life circumstances led Doris on to a downward spiral of alcoholism. She lost her faith and nearly her family. Kevin, who was six at the time of his father's death, became a big brother and the leader and protector of the family in many ways. He is a remarkable person!

Her kids have little memory about their father, have conflicting thoughts about him, and loved their stepdad as their real father. They chose to adopt his last name of Coupland instead of Kennedy. That saddened Mother and there is no one else to carry on the Kennedy name. But it is very understandable why they chose to do so. We lost contact with a couple of the kids for a while and that was hard for us Kennedy sisters not to be a part of their lives.

Getting back to Frank's murder, the investigation was a major media story for weeks but in the end all suspects, including his girlfriend, were questioned and released. They even brought the state police in to help solve the crime but to no avail.

Many years later, a police detective who was a young police officer when Frank was killed, revealed to me that Knipper had given a "death bed declaration" and confessed to the murder. According to the officer, Knipper and Frank were both seeing Miss London and he decided to off the competition and orchestrate the murder. Knipper set up Frank by having him drive an expensive pink Cadillac that night so the killers could identify him. Two pistols and a rifle were found in Knipper's car at his Modern Motor Sales lot.

The love triangle is only one theory. Another is that it was a gangster-affiliated loan shark revenge murder. It was a well-known fact that gangs were very involved in used cars in New Jersey. Others say it was a business double cross because Frank had had difficulties in a recent venture involving surplus Army jeeps.

In the late 1960s, a man saw Mildred and Jim walking and asked "Are you Mildred Kennedy?" She said, "Yes, I am." He told her, "Stay right here. I'll be right back with information about your brother Frank." But he never returned. That happened another time with a different man but he didn't return either.

Mother was at a loss to account for the shooting other than it must have been done "by some crazy kids celebrating New Year's Day" who might have done it on a dare. Police questioned many in the neighborhood and found several who had heard the shots. Daddy believed it was a case of mistaken identity.

I believe the real story might be that he was an ex-Marine and an ex-police officer and that he was somehow working undercover. The reason he left his wife and family was to protect them. The car lot clearly had mob/gangster affiliations. He was working there to uncover mob activity and that was why he was murdered. It is bizarre how the murder was never solved. How clear can it be? He was driving a pink Cadillac, was chased through town and shot... after the boss and girl had been dropped off!

A line in a newspaper story read: "The big question for the cops was why, the big task to find and apprehend who did it." Those questions are still unanswered. It remains an unsolved crime in the state of New Jersey after sixty years.

CHAPTER 7

THE HOBOKEN KENNEDY TRIO

Since the first two Kennedy boys died as babies, and now with Frank gone, it was just us three Kennedy girls. We still smile and remember our handsome, charming, playful, and mischievous brother, and we are forever saddened over the circumstances of his adult life. But as hard and difficult as it was to deal with Frank's death, we knew we had to keep going.

Mildred, Patty, and I were raised by a strict, no-nonsense, controlling mother, and a truly good, fun, and loving father. We were grounded in the Catholic faith and the foundations of faith, hope, and love. We are Depression-era girls and learned, through our upbringing, how to acknowledge and face the daily realities and hardships of World War II. Of course, Mildred saw firsthand the toll that took on the young men of our generation. We were aware of the realities of our time but we were still able to laugh at life. Our faith and life experiences helped us cope with Frank's shocking death.

We Kennedy girls have an unbreakable bond. We continue to be devoted to and love our children, and we raised them the best we knew how. We are separated from each other with Mildred on the East Coast and Patty on the West Coast and me wherever else in the country we are. But we are still Hoboken Kennedy sisters and we continue to be strong, resilient, hopeful, determined, compassionate, faithful, and loving.

Thankfully, Doris eventually kept going as well. In 1976, with the help of good friends, Doris entered rehabilitation and through Alcoholics Anonymous has been sober ever since. She regained faith and found strength and wisdom in

God to live soberly and well one day at a time. She became the mom she always desired to be, and she became a doting and loving grandmother.

While it would be years before the Hayes cousins would see Doris's boys much, Doris's daughter, Maureen, lived with Patty and Johnny for part of her high school years. Maureen, or "Little Mo" as she was called, was not a blood relative, but became a favorite of the Hayes kids, who loved her as a very special cousin. Johnny and Patty were good and loving to her. Doris herself became a favorite guest at Hayes children's weddings and other occasions, and her visits were anticipated and thoroughly enjoyed by Patty's family.

Mildred, Patty, and I married loving and devoted Irish husbands. They, in turn, feel very blessed to have us Kennedy girls as wives! Jim would say, "I thank God that I had five children and a great wife." The three Irish boys respected and appreciated each other as well. Johnny has great respect for Jim and Mick's service, thinks Jim was one of the nicest people he had ever met, and that Mick is quite the character and a lot of fun to be with. And Jim and Mick thought the best thing about Johnny is that he had married a saint. Johnny said, "I married the sweetest girl I ever met, the pretty girl at Todd. She is the best wife I could ever imagine, and she became the greatest mom there is." And I'm pretty sure Mick is still glad he followed through on his vow to "marry that girl" the first time he saw me across the cafeteria!

Hoboken is a nostalgic part of our past but it is no longer the blue-collar town we grew up in. How things have changed! It is now a hip place that some refer to as a "party town." Many yuppies, artists, and immigrants moved in and displaced longtime Hobokenites, who were slowly priced out. A large majority of the residents now work in Manhattan, so the average income is way above average. Fewer and fewer Hoboken residents speak with a Jersey accent, since the majority of them are not originally from New Jersey.

Gentrification spurred re-zoning that encouraged new construction on the former industrial sites on the waterfront. Empty lots were built on, and tenements like the ones we lived in became high-priced condominiums that can go for as high as one million dollars. Even Engine Company Number 5, where Marty Sinatra served as captain, is now a private residence. The house Frank Sinatra was born in at 415 Monroe Street is now a private parking lot. Leo's Grandevous, where he played pool, is now a spacious, popular Italian restaurant owned by Nick DePalam, the grandson of the original owner Leo DiTerlizzi.

Parking can be a problem but it is fortunately still a walkable town. There is lots to do on the waterfront now. There are great parks and still amazing views. The Hudson River Waterfront Walkway now links several green spaces. There is even free public kayaking. Global restaurants, bistros, and bars line Washington Street, which is still the main thoroughfare. There are unique shops along Willow Avenue, and there is now a Frank Sinatra Drive and a Frank Sinatra Walking Tour, which brings back all kinds of wonderful memories from our time growing up in Hoboken. St. Michael's High School had its last graduating class in 1986 and is now Mother Seton Elementary School.

Our kids are all grown and many of the grandchildren are as well. With Mick and me in nearby Arizona, I feel blessed that we are near Patty and Johnny again and can visit their family from time to time. Johnny treats me like his real sister and still teases me, and he and Mick are like brothers. Through the years, they have drunk beer (a few times too many) and watched sports and other television, as Johnny is amused by Mick yelling at the TV. We have had many memorable pinochle card and domino games with the dutiful Kennedy sisters, as Johnny calls us, against Johnny and Mick. They are truly fun times with lots of laughter and wonderful memories.

Mildred has overcome her fear of flying and she and Jim had some memorable trips to California. Since Jim's passing in 1997, Mildred has had more visits, although only the younger generations can keep up with her amazing nonstop energy and activity.

Jim's death was sudden and so sad but also after a proud and romantic moment with Mildred as he left for work. That morning, for the first time in a long time, he decided to wear his 4th Marine jacket. Just as she did when they first met, Mildred's face brightened when she saw him. She told him how handsome he looked and they kissed goodbye in an even more special way than normal. It was a beautiful morning together. Later that morning, he would die from a sudden heart attack while standing in line at TKTS in Times Square, on an errand for his boss.

We all mourned the sudden loss of our WWII hero and loving, good, and God-fearing man. Mildred and her children especially mourned. But as Mildred dealt with loss and loneliness, her typical determined spirit kicked in and she lives a full, energetic, and meaningful life. After Jim's death, Millie dusted off her trumpet and joined the Blawenburg Band, the Brook Orchestra, and the Raritan Valley Symphonic Band. In addition, she volunteers at the Hillsborough Police Department and the Social Service Department Hospital as well as at church. She continues to work as a nurse, devotes herself to her children and grandchildren, and roots for son Sean's highly successful high school football teams, while giving an earful to anyone who dares criticize him in the stands!

As our older Kennedys pass on, it means so much to us that the Kennedy grandchildren, and even great-grandchildren, have bridged physical distance as adults and continue to cherish an unmistakable and special bond with one another.

For example, while serving as a pilot in the Air Force, Matt, the youngest of the Hayes children, flew out of McGuire Air Force base in New Jersey and he and his wife Julie became very close with the Jersey Murphys. Their son, Ryan, and Sean's daughter, Kat, became best friends as toddlers and remain close even as Matt and Julie moved back to California. Kat is now an adopted California Hayes family member. Patty's son, Greg, and my son, Michael, reconnected through basketball in Beijing, China. My daughter, Kathleen, reconnected with the Hayes family living in Arizona and, through that connection, has made several trips to California. There are so many other examples of how the younger generations of Kennedys are truly family. They all wish they could see each other more but are thankful for social media. Their appreciation and love for each other is a blessed legacy of the Kennedys of Hoboken, and we are so thankful for it.

So it goes to this day. There is so much more to write about but there is no book big enough to contain all the stories we could tell about our children, our grandchildren, and now our great-grandchildren. There are many more stories about our church and community involvement, of the countless blessings we have received and the love we have shared. May this book be an inspiration to those who read it.

Mildred, Patty, and I remain Hoboken Kennedy sisters forever and are eternally blessed and grateful for that!

EPILOGUE

By James Murphy

T he story of the Kennedys of Hoboken is arguably as
much about the place they called home as it is about
the family. For almost sixty years, their universe was
affectionately known as the Mile Square City. Hoboken, New
Jersey sits on the western shores of the Hudson River, directly
across from midtown Manhattan. It was once a peninsula
when it was occupied by the Lenni Lenape Indians. But
time changed its landscape from being bucolic and sylvan
to a busy and densely populated urban area. It was in that
setting that Agnes and Patrick Kennedy decided to establish
residency and raise their four children.

Hoboken is within a few miles of Ellis Island. As
immigrants to the United States were processed at Ellis
Island and deemed suitable to enter the country, many
planted their roots in New York and New Jersey. Hoboken
was among those places where people from Europe felt that
they could pursue their dreams of a new life in America
while also preserving their customs and traditions.

During the time the Kennedys were living in Hoboken,
the city's population of between 50,000 and 60,000 was
mostly German, Italian, and Irish. In an area that small,
it was hard not to interact with others who looked a little
different, spoke a little different, and even dressed a
little different. People worked together, played together,
worshiped together, and socialized together. Ethnic customs
were showcased and enjoyed, especially during holidays.
My mom would often tell us about the solemn Italian
processions on Good Friday and "trick or treating" taking
place at Thanksgiving instead of Halloween. There would

be other stories she would share with us about growing up in Hoboken and as I listened I would find myself wishing I had grown up there too. In a way, that wish came true.

I had an opportunity to experience Hoboken in the fifties and sixties while my grandparents were still living there. My time there gave me a glimpse into what it was like growing up in Hoboken and imagining how Agnes and Patrick, along with their four children Mildred, Francis, Patricia, and Janet, were influenced by their surroundings. It is those indelibly fond memories which arouse feelings of joy and comfort.

My time in Hoboken was precious to me because of my grandfather. I was very close to him. I idolized him. The bond was undeniable. Outside of my parents, he was an enormous influence on me, so to spend time with him was always a joyful and fulfilling occasion. To do it on his turf in Hoboken made it especially significant for me.

My family lived in New Jersey. We were about twenty-five miles from Hoboken and living that close enabled us to visit often with my grandparents. On our drive in, I would think about how I could monopolize my grandfather. In the end, I knew better than to expect that of him. Selfish as it was, I knew he loved all of his grandchildren. I also knew that he would find a way to give each of my siblings an equal dose of his attention and time.

Being the oldest grandchild, I must confess I did get some extra bonus time with him. We would go to Yankees games together. I would take the bus into the Port Authority Building in mid-town Manhattan. My grandfather would be on the platform waiting for me. Knowing he was there filled me with much anticipation. We would take the subway to Yankee Stadium and before the game have a hot dog at one of the taverns across the street. I always remember sitting in box seats either along the third base line or behind home plate. Sitting in those locations pushed my grandfather further up on the pedestal of admiration that I deemed fitting for him. When the game was over, some ushers would line the infield, while others would open field-level gates.

Fans could walk out onto the playing field to access exits underneath the bleachers. My grandfather and I always took advantage of going out onto the field after a game. To be in center field in Yankee Stadium with my grandfather as we strolled past the monuments to Miller Huggins, Babe Ruth, and Lou Gehrig was undeniably a perfect end to a perfect day.

I had other bonus time opportunities with my grandfather. Most memorable were the walks we took together in Hoboken.

My grandfather enjoyed smoking cigars. Actually, he really didn't smoke them. It was more like he chewed on them. He didn't have many teeth. My grandmother objected to him "smoking" in their apartment. To appease her and to chew on that stogie, he'd take a walk. Since he was a police officer who "walked the beat," his cigar strolls usually took place when he worked 8 AM to 4 PM. He would have his dinner and then he'd head out, properly attired and always donning his fedora. I don't remember the brand of cigar he "smoked" but I'll never forget the humidor he kept them in and the aroma that lifted from it when he pried it open.

On days when we were visiting and on those special occasions when I would sleep over, I looked forward to our after-dinner walk. He had nicknames for his grandchildren. Mine was Duke. Once he finished his meal, he would reach for his hat and say, "Duke, let's go." I knew what that meant so there was no hesitation on my part. I was always ready and eagerly welcomed the opportunity to be seen with him and to have his full attention.

The route of the "walk" was somewhat predictable. It usually encompassed parts of his patrol beat. (He didn't drive so "he walked the beat.") As we left the apartment, I'd sidle up to him, proud to be in his company and honored to be his grandson. In my eyes, he was a celebrity.

When the weather was warm, Hobokenites would sit on their stoops, hoping to catch a cool breeze. TV was a new form of home entertainment then but was no substitute for gathering outside with family, friends, and neighbors. In many ways, the stoop served the same purpose as the town squares in Europe. It drew people together. As we strolled by, someone would yell "Hey Pat." He would reply with a cheerful "How ya' doin'." Hearing his name confirmed my sense of his popularity.

I remember being out on one of our walks when someone came up to my grandfather to let him know that some kids in the neighborhood were being mischievous and involved in behavior that could morph into something more serious. My grandfather always carried his police notebook. He made a notation regarding the "intelligence" and thanked the person for the information. This was community policing at its best. The exchange was also something more significant. It was an example of trust and respect. Here was this citizen trusting and respecting my grandfather, knowing that he would take appropriate action without betraying his source. My grandfather expressed his gratitude and we continued on our walk. He didn't say much after that. He didn't have to. I witnessed him at his best. Doing what he loved, dedicated to his craft and determined to keep his city safe.

My grandfather taught me many lessons about respect, compassion, kindness, and not rushing to judgment. He did so by his actions. A very vivid memory also took place during a walk. It was a Saturday. I think he had the day off. After lunch, we headed out, seeking the familiarity of the streets of Hoboken. That particular day, we stopped at a tavern on the corner of Washington and Fourteenth Streets. He knew the area well. He did traffic on that corner. He knew all of the merchants who operated a variety of shops and businesses within a four-block radius. My grandfather liked this place and he knew the owner. As we walked in, there were three or four men sitting at a table. They were loud. I was probably ten or eleven and a little frightened by their behavior. When the owner spotted us entering his establishment, he immediately approached my grandfather. He whispered something to him while pointing in the direction of this group. My grandfather went over to the men and spoke to them. The mood of the table changed. He took me by my hand to the bar, where he ordered a glass of whiskey and a coke for me. After about fifteen minutes, he said to me, "Stay here Duke; I'll only be a few minutes." He walked over to the group and without saying a word they rose from their chairs and followed him out of the tavern. I would learn later that my grandfather took the men across the street to the YMCA. Out of his pocket, he paid for rooms for them. What I also learned later is that the tavern owner wanted my grandfather to call "downtown" and request a paddy wagon. Gramps balked at that idea and assured the owner that he would take care of the matter in his way. That's what he did.

My journeys through the streets of Hoboken gave me insights into the values embraced by the Kennedy family. There were no class distinctions there. Everybody seemed the same to me, which in retrospect meant that they were all middle class folks, working hard, trying to make ends meet and buoyed by the little things like a drink with friends, a summer night on the stoop, a stick ball game in the street, a wedding, a birthday, or just spending some time in one of Hoboken's small parks. It was a Norman Rockwell painting waiting to happen. I liked what I saw. It felt safe. The people were friendly. As my mom, Mildred, used to say, "Everybody got along." It sure seemed that way.

As I walked the streets with my grandfather, I didn't sense any hostility or any tension. People just seemed to be content with what they had and were happy for others when they got a break or had something nice happen in their lives. Not everyone had an automobile so the principal means of transportation was a pair of shoes. "We walked everywhere," according to my mom. She walked to school, walked to church, walked to the stores, and walked to the movies. That was true for most everyone else in Hoboken and it seemed true when I was out with my grandfather. The opportunities for social interaction were boundless and I think that condition cemented their sense of community.

It also provided a bridge between ethnic groups as people from different parts of Europe realized that their common bond was the values they shared. That commonality defined Hoboken.

When I reflect about my grandparents, my mom, my aunt Patty, my aunt Janet, and my Uncle Frank, I'm struck by the values which they subscribed to and embraced. They were hardworking, dedicated to their families, patriotic, generous, compassionate, kind, selfless, tolerant, and most of all, loving people. They grew up in an environment where those values were nurtured and modeled. How great is that! What is even greater is that the Kennedys and other Hobokenites not only passed those values on to their children but they continued to live them and serve as examples to others.

I can say with unequivocal certainty that I have been shaped by the Kennedy values and by my time in Hoboken. I have tried in earnest to pass those on to my children with the expectation that the Kennedy values can lead to more fulfilling lives for them. In so doing, this story of the Kennedys of Hoboken can continue through them.

ACKNOWLEDGEMENTS

I loved my Aunt Janet! She is one of my favorite people ever and she brought laughter, honesty, passion, joy, faith, and love to our family. I have wonderful memories of her: making me smile when I was a second-grader on the way back from solemnly receiving communion in church, her laughing through tears of frustration while trying to make homemade ravioli; her loud, animated, and loving conversations with Uncle Mick; and in July 2008 the support and love she showed Mom during last few days of Mom's life. She led our family in prayer as we surrounded Mom's hospital bed, when Mom was so truly peaceful and beautiful.

I loved listening to Aunt Janet tell stories of growing up in Hoboken. One day, I asked her if she would write down her stories. She agreed and wrote a book full of them! She called it "Growing up in Hoboken."

A few months after Dad's passing at ninety-two on June 28, 2018, I sent Aunt Janet's "Growing Up In Hoboken" to my family. My daughter Kara was so impressed with it that I asked my cousin Colleen, Aunt Janet's daughter, if I could publish it. She said yes and then she became an invaluable source of information, insight, and encouragement.

I expanded and added to Aunt Janet's writings with information and stories from letters Grandmother Kennedy wrote, a Kennedy Hoboken sisters interview by brother Tom at our parents' wonderful 50th wedding anniversary party, love letters between Dad's parents, a book that Aunt Doris wrote but never published, newspaper clippings and video interviews of my wonderful godparents Mildred and Jim Murphy, and firsthand recollections of Dad, Uncle Mick, Aunt Patsy, Uncle Mike, and my Jersey cousins.

As I wrote the book, my admiration, appreciation, and love for my parents and relatives grew deeper. I wish that I could somehow fully express my gratitude to them.

Aunt Janet died on May 28, 2012, and is interred at Arlington National Cemetery. Family members and Kennedy relatives attended the beautiful and moving ceremony on September 13, 2012.

Colleen passed along a letter that Dad wrote to Uncle Mick after Aunt Janet's passing. Both of them thought they would go first, not their wives, who they loved so much. He wrote: "This is a note I never expected to write. My admiration for you is boundless. I loved Janet as a sister, not as an in-law. Janet and Patty are together again. If they are not in Heaven together, none of us stand a chance. You and I are two of the luckiest Irishmen on earth for having been blessed with marriage to two remarkable women and mothers. We miss them dearly and our love for them continues to grow ad infinitum." This is how my father felt about Mildred and Jim as well.

Ultimately, this is a story about the three Kennedy sisters, the Hoboken Kennedy Trio, who became devoted and loving wives, mothers, grandmothers, and great-grandmothers. They affected their communities and church in significant ways and left a rich legacy of faith, hope, and love. This book is a testimony to that legacy.

Thanks to:

Dave Haberer: For the cover and interior book design.

Suzan Frierson: I am thrilled and grateful that Suzan served such an important role in the book as manuscript editor. Someday she needs to write her own book about the Friersons and her wonderful grandparents Ed and Bettye, who have been an inspiration to me and my own family. Her dad Eddie's books about Christy Mathewson inspired this book.

West Ranch Wildcats Natalie Jawher, Chase Neelley, Jenna Rorick, and Ryan Tucker: They have been a pleasure to teach and I am forever grateful for their willing and skillful work on the book.

Grandma Kennedy: She loved and prayed for each of her grandchildren, and made many clothes for us! Most of all, she left an example of devotion to faith and family.

Grandpa Kennedy: He was the coolest, most loving, and best grandfather any kid could ask for. He could make me laugh no matter what my mood. He taught me by example how to love even when mistreated, especially at times by my grandmother!

My godparents Aunt Mildred and Uncle Jim: They are two of my heroes and shining examples in life. One of my biggest regrets in life is not getting to spend enough time with Uncle Jim. One of my greatest joys is time spent with Aunt Mildred.

Brian Hayes: My big brother who would do anything to help others. I wish I could have spoken to him about this book because he would have remembered so much.

Aunt Doris: She became a beloved and special aunt to the Hayes family. Mom and Doris made up for lost time as Mom treated Doris as her true sister-in-law, both cherished and loved.

Colleen Murphy Strother: My sweet younger cousin growing up and now an inspiration in faith, character, and love. She passed along priceless memories from her dad, Uncle Mick, and told them as her mom would have. She added this poignant thought: "I'm sure our moms know the truth now about Frank. I hope handsome Uncle Frank has some peace and that his sons know he loved them."

Uncle Mick: I smile when I think of him. Like Dad, he got better with age and loved his wife above all else. The best I ever golfed was with him because he was so patient and wise, and our house was never more alive than when he was sitting in the living room watching TV.

The Jersey Kennedy granddaughters Erin, Maureen, Kat, and Meghan: They reflect the goodness, spirit, and beauty of their Grandmother "Millie" Murphy.

All my Kennedy cousins: Memories with them are among the most cherished of my life and we keep building more. The bond we share as Kennedys is a testimony to our mothers' love and faith.

Jimmy Murphy: He is the former Chief Deputy of the United States District Court of the District of New Jersey. He set a high standard for the rest of us Kennedy grandchildren. He was like a big brother to me during my junior high and early high school years and he remains a role model and inspiration. When I am with him, I feel a link to Mom and Grandpa Kennedy. Jimmy's insightful epilogue shows that the Kennedys of Hoboken are relevant today because of their timeless values and wisdom.

Delaney Patricia Hayes: The youngest of the Hayes grandchildren is my precious, beautiful, intelligent, funny, and loving goddaughter. To quote Poppa – "Love you more."

Sons-in-law Tim and Jeremy: Both are uniquely gifted and I find peace in knowing their deep love and devotion to my daughters. They both are truly answers to lifelong prayers. I am thankful to call them friends and that they like the Kennedy lasagna!

Megan and Kara: They are the greatest joys and blessings of my life and make me better through their goodness, spirit, character, love, and beautiful hearts. I am thankful they are such talented writers and for their corrections and suggestions to make this book better. Both honored, cherished, and loved their grandparents and older relatives and I am so thankful they reflect their Grandmother Hayes' heart, faith, integrity, and beauty.

The Hayes family: Our wonderful spouses, the grandchildren, and great-grandchildren have made us original ten kids even better, especially our sisters-in-law, granddaughters, and great-granddaughters. There is nothing much better than when the entire family is together.

Mom and Dad: They lovingly sacrificed so much for us. Their love and devotion to each other and the faith they inspired in us are their greatest gifts to our family. We lost Mom way too soon but we cherish that we had Dad for so long. As Dad would say, Mom is the inspiration for our family. That is why of the five Hayes boys who have daughters, four of us and our wives named one of our daughters in honor of our Mom, Patricia Marie Kennedy Hayes: Karen Marie, Lisa Marie, Kara Marie, and Delaney Patricia.

Almighty and Eternal God: Most of all and above all else, thanks to our loving Father in generations past and generations to come for a cup that overflows with blessings. His timeless and boundless love, grace, and mercy, through the life, death, and resurrection of Christ, provide eternal hope that the Kennedys of Hoboken are reunited in Heaven and that we will see them again.

KENNEDY LASAGNA RECIPE

The Kennedy sisters' legacy lives on in many ways. A special one is through the Kennedy lasagna recipe, passed down through the generations. It is a staple at Hayes Christmas Eve celebrations wherever we are. The Hayes family all agree it is the best lasagna made anywhere in the world! We also know that no one ever made it better than Mom because her love is the one ingredient that is impossible to replace.

Sauce
- 1 lb. of ground beef or sausage (optional)
- 1 large onion, chopped
- 1 lb. mushrooms, sliced
- 1-4 cloves of Garlic (optional)
- 1 large package of Lawry's or Schillings spaghetti mix
- 28 oz. of tomato puree
- 28 oz. of tomato sauce
- 12 oz. of tomato paste

Brown ground beef in a frying pan. Pour contents into a crock-pot or large pot. Sauté the onion until soft. Add mushrooms and sauté until soft. Add onions and mushrooms to the pot. Add remaining ingredients to the pot and simmer on low heat for many hours. Stir occasionally.

Lasagna
- 1 box of Lasagna noodles
- 15 oz. of Ricotta cheese
- 16 oz. of Mozzarella cheese
- 1 egg
- Parmesan cheese

Preheat oven 350 degrees Fahrenheit.

Cook noodles. Mix egg with Ricotta cheese in bowl. Thinly slice mozzarella cheese.

Lightly coat the bottom of a 13" x 9" pan with sauce. Layer the noodles to cover the sauce. Cover the noodles with 1/3 of the Ricotta mixture and then 1/3 of the Mozzarella cheese. Cover with a layer of sauce. Repeat TWICE more with the noodles, cheeses, and sauce.

Sprinkle Parmesan cheese over the top. Bake in the oven for at least 30 minutes. Let it sit at least 20 minutes before cutting. The longer it sits the better it will set and make it easier to get out of the pan.
Special ingredient ... unlimited amounts of LOVE!

About the Authors

Janet Murphy lived a rich life as a Navy WAVE, mother, grandmother, and great-grandmother until her passing in June 2012. She is interred at Arlington National Cemetery. Her memoir "Growing up in Hoboken" is the basis for the book.

Greg Hayes is the nephew of Janet Murphy and attended UCLA, where he received a BA in History and Master's Degree in Educational Administration. He is the author of *Camp with Coach Wooden*.

On Facebook:

 The Kennedys of Hoboken - by Janet Murphy and Greg Hayes

 Pat and John Hayes Scholarship Fund

 PAT AND JOHN HAYES SCHOLARSHIP FUND: The scholarship honors the lives and service of Pat and John Hayes and is awarded to a deserving high school senior who has excelled in community service while in high school. For more information and to donate to the scholarship, please visit the Pat and John Hayes Scholarship page on Facebook.

Made in the USA
San Bernardino, CA
07 September 2019